Chris Martin has est ... foremost Christian thinkers w ... logies in general, and the social internet in particular. In this book, he demonstrates why it is so important for Christians to think well about these world-changing, heart-shaping, soul-forming technologies. I highly recommend this book to anyone who wants to better understand how we can take back what they've so eagerly taken from us.

Tim Challies, author and blogger

With great insight, Chris shows us how the social internet we carry around in our pockets has shaped the world and is shaping us. If you hold angst for the alarming and adverse impacts of social media, this book will give language to your concerns and provide hopeful and helpful solutions. Chris's wise counsel to admire beauty, walk in humility, and value silence and accountability is an important challenge for all of us, including parents, ministry leaders, teachers, and anyone who in a role to influence others.

Eric Geiger, senior pastor, Mariners Church

The internet may be financially free, but it has other costs. In *Terms of Service*, Chris Martin skillfully unpacks the trade-offs of life in the digital age—helping us become more attentive to the hidden costs of the social internet. This is a valuable read for any Christian who spends significant amounts of time online—which is pretty much all of us these days. We're aware of the ways the social internet is remaking the world. But are we alert to the ways it is remaking us? This book helps us carefully consider this question, and gives us tools for moving forward in health.

Brett McCracken, senior editor at
The Gospel Coalition, author of *The Wisdom Pyramid:
Feeding Your Soul in a Post-Truth World*

Terms of Service is a terrifying book—which is exactly why you must read it. With charity and clear-headedness, Chris Martin guides us through the world that we all inhabit but few of us understand. His personal knowledge and extended study of how the internet is shaping us will benefit pastors, parents, and anyone who cares of about the discipleship of souls. So put down your phone and pick up this book.

Hannah Anderson, author of *All That's Good: Recovering the Lost Art of Discernment*

Terms of Service will annoy you. If you are already reaping the neurochemical rewards of the social media echo chambers of your own choosing, I recommend that you do not read this book. Who reads books anymore anyways? I mean, if it is longer than 280 characters, why would any . . .

Read Mercer Schuchardt, associate professor of communication, Wheaton College, PhD, New York University under Neil Postman, bestselling author of *Amusing Ourselves to Death*

If anyone should write the book on how social media (or the "social internet," as Chris so wisely calls it) has affected us all, it's Chris Martin. He has been in the trenches of social media for over a decade and observed what's going on from that vantage point, not an ivory tower. *Terms of Service* will help anyone looking to understand how and why our online behaviors have shaped us and what it means to move forward in a digital world with a kingdom mindset.

Julie Masson, director of External Engagement, Ethics & Religious Liberty Commission

It's not hard to offer negative critiques of the social internet. What is hard is giving sustained attention to those problems and following it with sound guidance on how to live faithfully in the real world. Chris's years of experience in digital ministry and careful personal practices make him a worthy guide.

John Dyer, professor and VP of Educational Technology, Dallas Theological Seminary, author of *From the Garden to the City: The Place of Technology in the Story of God*

TERMS
OF
SERVICE

TERMS
OF
SERVICE

THE REAL COST OF SOCIAL MEDIA

CHRIS MARTIN

PUBLISHING
NASHVILLE, TENNESSEE

For Magnolia Grace.
This is why.

Acknowledgments

First and foremost, I need to thank my friend and colleague Trillia Newbell. Her friendly prodding led me to dust off an old notebook with a social media book outline sketched in the back. This book wouldn't exist if it weren't for her keen eye and dear friendship. Of course, I also need to thank Taylor Combs and the team at B&H for believing in this project and doing all the hard work to bring it to life.

Thank you, Susie, for your support and patience as I worked on this project. Given that most of it was written during the pandemic, it's not like we had a lot going on except for, well, parenting a newborn.

Thank you to Tracey and Josie Bowler, Jesse and Sara Poarch, Brandon and Christa Smith, Elizabeth and Zach Edwards, Bayleigh Harvey, David Drobny, Trevor Atwood, Jeremy Young, Dustin Walker, and Elisha Lawrence for not only your friendship but also your willingness to review the earliest version of this book. Your feedback was helpful.

Now, a note of thanks to a wide assortment of people without whom this book would not exist. Thank you to my amazing parents, Joe and Catherine Martin. Thank you to John Houser, Russ Isaacs, Pamela O'Reilly, Donna Roof, Jason Birkenbeul, Greg MaGee, Bill Heth, and so many other treasured teachers whose investment long ago led to this project. Finally, a posthumous thank you to Neil Postman, whose work in *Amusing Ourselves to Death* inspired not only this book but has formed my mind more than any book short of Scripture itself.

Contents

Part 3: Where Do We Go from Here?

Introduction

This is a book about fish.

Not literally but metaphorically.

David Foster Wallace, American author and novelist, once wrote: "There are these two young fish swimming along and they happen to meet an older fish swimming the other way, who nods at them and says, 'Morning, boys. How's the water?' And the two young fish swim on for a bit, and then eventually one of them looks over at the other and goes, '"What's water?"'"[1]

The "moral" of this parable, if you will, is that most people are not aware of certain features of the world around them, despite how intertwined those features are in their lives. This is my attempt to be the older fish, except I am not asking you how the water is. I'm here to tell you that the water is poisoned.

My fear is that most people who use social media are like the two young fish in David Foster Wallace's parable. Social media has become so woven into all of our lives that, like a fish in water, we don't even notice it anymore. We just consume content on social media constantly without ever stopping to consider the puppet strings that are being pulled behind all the content on our screens. We consume content and content consumes us. This is my plea for you to stop scrolling for a moment and consider the state of the pixelated water in which you swim.

We easily swim through our lives today without considering the effects of social media on ourselves and the world around us. We spend our Friday nights scrolling Instagram while watching Netflix, and we don't even think twice about it. We fight with strangers about politics on Twitter *because it's just what you do.* We post pictures of our loved ones and life updates to Facebook without even considering the privacy implications of posting that information.

I grew up on social media, using AOL Instant Messenger as early as the first grade. I have spent about ten years deep-sea diving in this ocean by merit of my daily work and personal study. This is my attempt to steal your attention away from the Silicon Valley geniuses who have spent their lives trying to harness it so I can alert you to just how harmful it may be for your heart and your mind.

The social internet is brilliant and obscene. It sharpens the mind and dulls it. It brings nations together and tears them apart. It perpetuates, reveals, and attempts to repair injustice. It is an untamed beast upon which we can only hope to ride but never quite tame. It is hard to see it now, but the social internet is not just the latest iteration of the printing press or the television. The pervasiveness and invasiveness of the social internet can be likened to an alien invasion. You can't stop it;

you must learn to live alongside it, whether you like it or not. You may delete your Facebook account, but a friend will ask you if you have one. You can stay off Twitter, but you will hear about what happened there on the evening news.

We may be able to log off the social internet, delete our accounts, and never participate, but we can never escape its influence. What is it doing to us?

What's the Point?

You can easily become discouraged when you are exploring the depth of negativity wrought by social media and our relationship with it. Whether it's the rampant privacy concerns that average users ignore or the mental health effects that go untreated or the blurring of the line between "truth" and "fiction," when you start to notice the toxins in the water and no one else seems to care, it can be disorienting to the point of despair. This is why I have kept the "What's the point?" question at the fore of my mind all along.

My goal is not to tell you to delete your social media accounts. Though that is a fine application of what you will read. Nor is the point of this to call out the unethical practices of social media companies in their perpetual harvesting of user data for profit. Though that does happen in here.

So then, what *is* the point of this book?

The point is simply to help you see that the water is toxic. The goal is to help you recognize that social media is changing the way you think, feel, and live. Like water to a fish, social media has come to pervade the lives of everyone. As a fish cannot live apart from water, we cannot live apart from social media, even if we delete our accounts! My grandma has never used social media in her life. She might read this book because she loves me, but this book will be utter nonsense to her because she has never logged onto any social media platform. Guess what, though: in our weekly phone calls, she often mentions something her friends saw on Facebook. Social media is inescapable.

Because we cannot escape social media, my goal is not to call you to delete your accounts and log off. I simply want you to recognize that social media is changing how you think and feel about life and largely in negative ways. Whether this book leads you to delete your accounts or use them with greater discernment and care doesn't matter to me. My hope is that your perspective is reoriented enough to at least examine your relationship with social media and not simply scroll on mental autopilot anymore. I provide some action steps in part 3, but those are optional applications of a bigger purpose: to *know* that the water is toxic.

In order to accomplish that purpose, though, I need something from you.

What This Book Requires of You

In his book *Amusing Ourselves to Death*, Neil Postman writes about Lewis Mumford, a twentieth-century American writer and thinker:

Lewis Mumford . . . has been one of our great noticers. He is not the sort of a man who looks at a clock merely to see what time it is. Not that he lacks interest in the content of clocks, which is of concern to everyone from moment to moment, but he is far more interested in how a clock creates the idea of "moment to moment."

"The clock," Mumford has concluded, "is a piece of power machinery whose 'product' is seconds and minutes." In manufacturing such a product, the clock has the effect of disassociating time from human events and thus nourishes the belief in an independent world of measurable sequences.

Moment to moment, it turns out, is not God's conception, or nature's. It is man conversing with himself about and through a piece of machinery he created.

In Mumford's great book *Technics and Civilization*, he shows how, beginning in the fourteenth century, the clock made us into time-keepers, and then time-savers, and now time-servers.[2]

If my book is to accomplish its purpose, to get you to recognize the noxious nature of the social media waters in which we swim, I need you to help me by being a "great noticer" like Lewis Mumford.

The product of a clock is its seconds and minutes; the product of social media is the content we consume. Like Mumford looked beyond the seconds and minutes produced by the clock, so we must look beyond the funny cat videos and family photos produced by our Facebook feeds. Man made the clock to serve man, but man ended up serving the clock. Man made social media to serve man, but man has come to serve social media.

I will serve you better if you read this book with the mind of Lewis Mumford, attempting to be a "great noticer" who looks beyond the surface of our most consuming pastime to the depths of how it is affecting every facet of our lives.

Also, before we go any further, we have to do a bit of housekeeping in regard to terminology. I will use the term *social internet* more frequently than *social media*. I do this because I want us to think of the entire internet as social, not just the *social media apps* that litter our phone screens. The principles here apply to all the ways we interact with people online, not just through Facebook, Instagram, or other such platforms. Generally, I will use the term *social media* when I am referring to the apps and platforms we all use, and I will use the term *social internet* if I am speaking more broadly of all

> Man made social media to serve man, but man has come to serve social media.

the ways the internet is social. If the term *social internet* trips you up, just mentally substitute *social media* for it; it's not a big deal. But, given that this book is meant to broaden our understanding of the social aspects of the internet and how we are changed by them, I think it is important that we think in terms of the social *internet*, not just social *media*.

The Terms of Service

Nobody reads the terms of service for new websites or software they sign up to use. For instance, if you're a Spotify user, when you checked the box in agreement with their terms, you provided them access to your photos and videos. Most Spotify users don't know that. Apple iTunes users, your terms indicate that you cannot use iTunes to construct a nuclear missile, so don't get any ideas! The terms of service (or terms and conditions, which is the same concept) to which we all agree when we sign up for a social media platform are often concerning in and of themselves.

We agree to a lot of conditions when we use social media that are not included in the terms of service we dishonestly say we have read when we sign up for these platforms. The terms of service we lie about reading do not mention the risk of mental illness or the insidious nature of cancel culture. There is no warning in terms of service agreements about rampant polarization or disfigured ideas of beauty.

When we chain ourselves to our preferred social media platforms, we give up more than we realize. Social media may not cost anything, but it isn't free.

I am concerned about the terms of our service to an invention that was originally designed to serve *us* but which *we have come to serve.* We are servants of the social internet. It governs our days and poisons our lives more than we recognize.

To what have we agreed? These social media apps may be free, but what do they *actually* cost us?

Let's find out.

PART 1

How We Got Here

CHAPTER 1

How Did the Social Internet Evolve?

'm a typical white, suburban, nineties kid. I was born in 1990 to Joe and Catherine Martin. My mom worked at a doctor's office early in my life but was soon at home being a full-time mom to me and eventually my brother, who was born in 1993.

My dad worked for IBM my entire childhood, and he spent most of that time working from home. Because my dad worked for IBM from home, we had a home computer before most of my friends at school did, or at least it felt that way. Working from home was so novel in the early nineties that a local newspaper came to our house and did a story on my dad's work-from-home setup, complete with a picture of me sitting on his lap in front of his chunky PC. I remember logging onto our beige-boxed Windows 95 IBM machine and heading straight to www.nick.com, Nickelodeon's website, to see what the website of my favorite TV channel looked like. I also remember my mom asking me to "please get off the internet" when she was expecting a phone call and I was busy collecting virtual trading cards of my favorite Nickelodeon characters—similar to how I was collecting Pokémon cards off-line. Later in elementary and middle school, once the internet didn't clog up the phone line, I spent hours online nearly every day chatting with friends via AOL Instant Messenger (AIM), checking out peoples' Myspace pages, and playing video games.

All of us can recall some of our earliest experiences with the internet. Whether you were six years old, like me, or thirty-six years old, you likely remember what it was like when you first started exploring the virtual landscape of the World Wide Web.

For most of us, the first internet experiences we remember are social in nature. Sure, some of you may have first experienced the internet in college when you had to use it for a research paper. Others of you may have first used the internet to do some online shopping. But, for most of us, our first experiences with the internet were *social*. The most magical part about the internet was, and is, our ability to connect with other humans all around the world with different cultures, interests, and life experiences.

You and I may know where *our* stories begin with the internet, but where does the internet's story begin? Before we explore the modern-day social internet and its effects on us, I think we would be wise to spend a little bit of time studying some internet history to discover how we got where we are today.

When the Internet Began

The internet, even in its earliest, most primitive state, was meant to be social. The early prototype of the internet as we know it today was created as a government project in the late 1960s as a tool for more rapid communication during the Cold War, should an attack be made on the United States by the Soviet Union. The project was called the Advanced Research Projects Agency Network, or ARPANET for short. It was a pretty simple form of communication between two computers, one at UCLA and one at Stanford, but it revolutionized communication from its inception.

The earliest version of what we know today as email was created in 1965, before the ARPANET even came onto the scene. Users of a computer system at Massachusetts Institute of Technology shared files and messages on a single remote disk by accessing that disk via different computer terminals. However, Ray Tomlinson is often credited with "inventing email" because he was the first to send messages across a network (the ARPANET) in 1971. Tomlinson is the one who decided to use the "@" in email addresses to differentiate between the person to whom he was sending the message and the server receiving the file.

The creation of the ARPANET and the sending of the first modern(ish) email by Ray Tomlinson happened in pretty quick succession in the late 1960s and early 1970s. Lots of developments and advancements were made to the prehistoric internet throughout the 1970s and 1980s, including the ability for small networks of computers to connect to other small networks of computers, but the next major change to the ever-evolving internet came in 1989 through the work of Tim Berners-Lee.

Tim Berners-Lee was a contractor for CERN, the Swiss science and technology research facility, when he proposed a project to his boss that would take the computer connections already happening and combine them with "hypertext," to create the earliest form of a graphical user interface, which laid the foundation of an internet pretty similar to what we see today, relatively speaking. His boss approved of the project, and Berners-Lee created the first version of the World Wide Web, or our modern internet.

The World Wide Web, from which we get the "www" that has historically preceded website URLs, made it so that anyone can set up a server, host a website, and travel between websites. Before, only individual computers or networks of computers could communicate. Now, with the World Wide Web, individual people who were not computer scientists could access the internet with basic web browsers on computers that didn't take years of training to operate.

The creation of the World Wide Web is regarded by many as the most important technological advancement in the twentieth century and perhaps modern history. It laid the groundwork for the modern internet. But before we examine the status of the internet as it is today, we need to explore what happened when the internet moved from government projects and university computer labs into our homes.

When the Internet Invaded Our Homes

With the creation of the World Wide Web, Tim Berners-Lee made the internet accessible to the masses. The internet was no longer a project reserved for government programs or university science projects. At the same time, Bill Gates was leading his company, Microsoft, to make computers accessible to the masses.

When Microsoft began creating easy-to-use operating systems and loading them onto desktop personal computers in the 1990s, home computer use skyrocketed. In 1991, *InfoWorld* reported that Microsoft sold four million copies of its Microsoft 3.0 operating system in its first year.[1] Those sales were impressive for the time, to be sure. Then, in 1995, *Popular Science* reported that Windows 95 sold forty million copies of its operating system in the first year it was available.[2] The internet invaded the home in 1995 in large part because the *computer* invaded the home in 1995. Without the easy-to-use, widely available Windows 95 operating system, the internet would not have made it into nearly as many homes as quickly as it did.

When the internet first invaded our homes in the mid to late 1990s, most people accessed it with a handful of different services that curated the internet for users, rather than letting users browse the internet freely like we do today; these services were called "walled gardens." The most widely used walled garden internet services in the 1990s were CompuServe, Prodigy, and America Online (AOL). CompuServe was for the more technically savvy and was the first widely available internet service, eventually purchased by H&R Block (yes, the tax company). It wasn't very pleasing to the eye, and it never became widely popular because it was difficult to use for the average person. Prodigy and AOL were both for the more popular-level internet user and, thus, had a wider appeal in the long run than did CompuServe. Prodigy was a project shared by CBS, Sears, and IBM. The three companies hoped they could use Prodigy to deliver news from CBS, drive online shopping for Sears, and harness attention in order to sell it to advertisers—one of the earliest attempts at the practice which pervades the internet today.

AOL eventually dominated Prodigy and CompuServe, driving the former to shut down and eventually acquiring the latter. AOL became the dominant way Americans logged onto the internet in the nineties for a number of reasons. Namely, it was easy to use, it mailed millions of free trial discs, and, most of all, it emphasized the social connection afforded by the World Wide Web. Tim Wu writes in *The Attention Merchants*: "AOL had, over the 1990s, decisively proven that the surest allure of the new computer networks was social—the prospect of interacting with other people."[3] CompuServe may have been first onto the consumer internet scene. Prodigy may have had shopping and been the first widely popular internet service. But AOL was the first to offer easy-to-use internet for the masses that celebrated the social aspect of this novel phenomenon. Its emphasis on the social is what made AOL define a generation of internet use.

AOL quickly became known for its iconic "You've got mail!" message delivered to users with new email upon log-on, so much so that a Tom Hanks movie was eventually built on the motto.[4] Beyond that, much of the allure of AOL revolved around its wide array of chat rooms, organized in a variety of ways: entertainment interests, cultural backgrounds, sexual preferences, and more. What AOL figured out in the nineties that other platforms struggled to understand was that what drew people to the internet wasn't the fancy features of a particular internet service provider but the ability to interact with other people. AOL dominated the internet in the nineties because it got out of the way, compared to other platforms, and provided a playground for people to interact with other people. As Joanne McNeil writes of AOL's role in the early days of the modern, social internet, "AOL was as much training wheels for the internet as it was a gateway drug to full-on internet addiction."[5]

Eventually, around 2001, AOL began to lose traction as dial-up was phasing out and faster, broadband internet became the norm. More standard web browsers like you see today became the primary way internet users engaged online. Instead of hanging out in the AOL user interface, users were opening Netscape Navigator, Internet Explorer, or another early web browser and "surfing the web" on their own. Millions of internet users who had been self-confined to the AOL ecosystem were now leaving their walled garden and exploring the wider internet, beyond AOL chat rooms and key-word searches. These internet users still wanted to be social, but it would look a bit different now.

Enter: early, modern social media platforms.

The Precursors to Our Modern Social Internet

The two earliest modern social media platforms were GeoCities and Friendster, and each had its own solid community. The two were built a bit differently. GeoCities, most popular in the late 1990s, was a more geographically focused social media platform that centered community around literal cities, as you could guess by its name. It allowed users to create groups of web pages that were organized geographically. Users congregated around those web pages and built communities that were often connected to the cities around which they were virtually gathered. It eventually sold to Yahoo! in 1999 and lost traction slowly over the next few years as Friendster exploded in popularity.

Friendster, which hit its peak popularity in 2003, is much more like our modern social media platforms than anything that came before it. The purpose of Friendster was simply to give people a place to connect with their friends, and strangers, online. It had no city-focused gimmick like GeoCities. Ironically, what killed Friendster was its popularity. The company could not keep up with the demand its users were putting on its servers, which resulted in slow-loading pages, frequent crashes, and ultimately a mass exodus from the service.

In the social vacuum being created by a malfunctioning Friendster, yet another social media platform was entering the scene, and it would be the most successful yet.

Myspace could accurately be called a "Friendster clone." It was created by a few employees of an internet marketing company who used Friendster, saw its many flaws, and thought they could do better. They took the best features of Friendster and made a more reliable service to scratch the same itch. It worked.

Myspace was started in 2003, the year Friendster was at its peak popularity, and by the next year it had overtaken Friendster in user base. Myspace, being a Friendster clone, was built with the same goals as Friendster—to connect people online—but it was more reliable and included a tight relationship with the music industry, which was a huge perk.

Myspace was the first social media platform I used beyond AOL Instant Messenger (AIM), which was just a messaging service. When it launched, Myspace didn't have an instant messaging component, so middle schoolers like me would often use Myspace to build our online personas while simultaneously communicating instantly with friends through AIM. By far the three biggest perks of Myspace for a teenage social media user like me were: (1) the ability to customize my profile page entirely; (2) the ability to rank my friends via Myspace's "top friends" feature; and (3) the ability to add a song to my profile page.

Myspace, through its profile page customization and music features, generated a form of personal expression that even current social media platforms don't possess. You can add whatever content you want to your Facebook or Instagram profiles, but you can't customize how the page actually *looks*. That was a huge deal for moody middle and high schoolers who wanted every part of their social media platform to be a means expressing their inner teenage angst.

Today's modern social media platforms are stages on which we can perform. Myspace gave users the ability to design the stage to their liking. That was revolutionary and unique.

In February 2005, Myspace CEO Chris DeWolfe had a meeting with the founder of an upstart social media company called Facebook. DeWolfe and Mark Zuckerberg had a conversation about merging Myspace, the most popular website in history, and Zuckerberg's new Facebook project. Zuckerberg wanted $75 million in the merger. DeWolfe declined. After a rocky middle of 2005 for Myspace, the two had a conversation again in the fall—Zuckerberg now wanted $750 million. DeWolfe, again, declined.

> Today's modern social media platforms are stages on which we can perform.

At its peak in early 2006, Myspace had 100 million accounts on its platform. It was seeing more visitors than Yahoo! and Google, two of the biggest websites at the time.

In July 2006 Myspace had 54 million unique visitors, but it would never get much better than that. Ultimately, Myspace would suffer from a litany of issues, the most pronounced of which was the mass exodus of young users from its platform to Zuckerberg's Facebook, once Facebook opened to users of all ages in September 2006. Myspace, despite being a more successful Friendster clone, would suffer the same fate as the platform it replaced—obsolescence at the hands of a hot, new platform young people loved.

The Modern Social Internet

Facebook was made available to anyone in the world aged thirteen or older in 2006, as it had previously only been available to anyone with an ".edu" email address.[6] Almost immediately, millions of users left Myspace and made Facebook their primary social media platform, myself included.

I remember hearing rumblings about Facebook when I was in high school before it was available for anyone not in college, so as soon as I was able to join, I did. Many of my high school friends did the same. Most of us maintained a Facebook and Myspace page simultaneously for a while, but within the first year or so of using Facebook, almost all of my friends had left Myspace entirely. For most social media users, Facebook replaced Myspace as their "primary" social media platform around 2006–2007. But another service was breaking out around that same time.

Twitter was created in 2006 by Jack Dorsey, Noah Glass, Biz Stone, and Evan Williams but didn't explode in popularity until the South by Southwest (SXSW) Interactive conference in 2007—not the first or the last hot start-up to gain traction at a SXSW event. Twitter was originally designed as an SMS-based (text-message-based) social media platform, designed for short, pointless messages. Where Facebook became the place for you to connect with *friends and family*, Twitter became the place for you to connect with *the world*.

Twitter quickly became a platform where everyday people could reach out to celebrities directly, where fans of a sport could interact around a big game like they were sitting next to each other in the stands, and where all other sorts of serendipitous interactions between people could occur, unlike on any other platform. I created my Twitter account in April 2008, my junior year of high school, just about a year after it debuted at SXSW Interactive, and used it to follow famous athletes, tech blogs, and other celebrities who were some of the earliest to the platform. Facebook felt like a virtual family reunion or party with friends. Twitter was a window to the wider world.

When the Internet Slipped into Our Pockets

Before we highlight a couple of other major social media platforms, we have to pause here in 2007–2008. Until this point, almost all social media was taking place on laptop or desktop computers. Smartphones existed and were widely used by businesspeople, but teens, the world's social media power users, were mostly still using flip phones, and their mobile communication was still primarily limited to texting and talking on the phone. The creation of our modern social media platforms was a seismic event unto itself; it allowed us to connect with our friends, our family, and the wider world in ways we never had before. But in 2007 social media experienced a dramatic shift that would massively amplify its influence.

When Steve Jobs announced the imminent release of the Apple iPhone on January 9, 2007, everything changed. Within the year the iPhone would release, and social media would jump from our desks into our pockets.

The iPhone revolutionized the social media industry, propelling it light-years forward, because of two major factors: (1) it made smartphones commercially popular beyond just businesspeople or wealthy teens, and (2) it led to social media being accessible anytime, anyplace. Soon a social media platform would be created specifically for the smartphone, unlike any social media platform had been before.

In 2009, Kevin Systrom and Mike Krieger created an app called Burbn. The app was a location check-in app similar to Foursquare. In fact, the app was *too* similar to Foursquare, which was dominant in the space at the time. Systrom and Krieger decided to redesign the app around the photo sharing feature, which was its most popular feature, and rebrand the app "Instagram," a mash-up of "instant camera" and "telegram." This new app launched in October 2010, and it quickly exploded in popularity.

Instagram was the first social media platform in which photos were the stars. Combine the fact that Instagram was made for iPhones, taking full advantage of their amazing-at-the-time cameras, and the photo-based nature of the app, and you have a pretty-easy-to-predict success story. Facebook bought Instagram for one billion dollars in 2012, and many believed Facebook overpaid. As of 2018, Bloomberg estimates that Instagram is worth $100 billion.[7] It has changed in many ways over the years, with its Snapchat-clone "Stories" function being its most revolutionary addition, but it has remained popular among a wide demographic of users, especially young women.

Lots of other social media platforms have been introduced in the smartphone era beyond those mentioned here, but we should conclude our short history of social media with a brief explanation of where we are today.

Where We Are Today

Today most people view social media as the following: Facebook, Instagram, Twitter, LinkedIn, Snapchat, and TikTok. Certainly other popular social media platforms exist, like Reddit and Pinterest, but they are not as widely used or considered in the mainstream.

Generally speaking, here is a brief explanation of how the platforms are viewed regarding their audiences and cultures:

- Facebook, the most widely used social media platform, is for the masses. Its most active users tend to be older than the primary users of other platforms. A lot of content that originates on other platforms eventually finds its way here.

- Instagram is viewed as the most positive, least toxic social media platform. Its most active users tend to be younger than Facebook's, but more in the millennial range than even Gen Z. It's known for polish, not authenticity. It is the "Facebook," or primary social media platform, for younger audiences.

- Twitter is the most niche of the major three early modern social media platforms. It has fewer users than Facebook and Instagram and tends to be adored by journalists in a variety of fields. It still maintains its "window to the world" vibe and is the primary place social media users congregate to communicate about world events. In terms of the ages of its user base, it is pretty diverse.

- LinkedIn is best understood as Facebook for businesspeople. Owned by Microsoft, it is a powerhouse in its own right but not for the masses. It is made fun of by many, but also the primary social media platform for many. It's like a professional networking event gone digital. Primarily older, professional audiences are here. It feels a bit like Facebook with a suit on.

- Snapchat is the dominant messaging app for young people. While technically a social media platform, it feels different from the others because of its emphasis on private messaging. It often feels more like an amped-up, image-driven messaging app with some traditional social media components. Typically made up of younger people, Instagram-age and younger.

- TikTok is the youngest social media platform out of all of these and the fastest growing. Owned by China-based ByteDance, TikTok is a video-based social media app that has quickly become the primary social media platform for Gen Zers. Its culture is unique. Its users are young. It will be around for a long time . . . unless more countries decide to ban it because of concerns about it being a China-based company.

Social media is ever-changing. Between the time this book is sent to print and the time you read it, there will surely be more platforms to add to this list. But what follows are applicable principles regardless of what social media platforms are popular when you read these words. Because when it comes down to it, no matter which name on the list is your preferred platform, social media platforms are all made of the same stuff: engaging content served to you for the purpose of modifying your behavior.

> Social media platforms are all made of the same stuff: engaging content served to you for the purpose of modifying your behavior.

CHAPTER 2

How Does the Social Internet Work?

There is no unringing the social internet bell. It is a Pandora's box that, now open, will never be closed. How many more clichés can I use to say it's here and it isn't going away?

We are stuck with the social internet whether we like it or not. It is not a fad, which I remember was a common refrain in the early 2010s, and its effects on our lives are far-reaching and often difficult to detect.

The internet has been social since its inception—the whole purpose from the beginning was to connect people via computers—and as long as the internet exists, people will use it to connect with other people. But the social internet as it exists today is a whole different animal from the social internet that existed as recently as the 1990s.

The social internet as we understand it is now much more than just connecting with people in AOL chat rooms who are interested in finding love or finding a website that hosts message boards all about the different aspects of deep-sea fishing. In those past social internet experiences, we felt completely in control of ourselves and when we chose to engage. We sat down and entered a chat room or logged into a favorite web forum. Today the social internet is far more invasive. We are always logged in. We are never off-line.

How does it work? Why do we keep coming back? Before we answer those questions, we need to first answer this question: Why did we start using the social internet to begin with?

Why Did We Start Using the Social Internet to Begin With?

As we just explored, the internet has been social since its beginning. It was originally a government project intended to connect military computers and eventually research institutions so they could communicate. But why did "normal people," people who weren't academics or techies, start engaging with the social internet? It wasn't just because AOL sent millions of discs to households around the world, encouraging them to sign up for a free trial. What was the appeal that not only got people to sign up for the internet but made them keep coming back? It depends on who you ask, but almost every answer revolves around the promise of community, exploration, and, at least at first, anonymity.

Anonymity

Before it became customary for some social media companies, like Facebook, to require a real name (or at least something that looked like a real name), the most popular corners of the social internet, like AOL communities or website message boards, required just a username. Users would regularly create and delete usernames, profiles, and content when they wanted to recreate themselves, casting themselves as a different character in the online universe.

Joanne McNeil, in her book *Lurking*, writes about what was so freeing in being identified by a username rather than your real name: "A username assumed the apprehension and ballast of a first impression; it was the skeleton that others on the internet had to start with to assemble a notion of your identity."[1] Donning a username and logging onto the social internet was like going to a costume party with thousands of people you didn't know and just a handful of people you did. Virtually zero social pressure existed in this anonymous environment. The worst-case scenario was that you would make a fool of yourself on one username, stop using it, and start up another one minutes later.

The idea that one could escape the troubles of the real world and pretend to be someone else entirely on the internet had quite an appeal, to say the least. I have clear memories of having a rough day in middle school—otherwise known as a "normal day" in middle school—and looking forward to going home, logging onto the internet, and assuming a different identity, totally disconnected from the awkward, nerdy kid I was stuck being at school every day. The early, anonymous days of the social internet provided a fantasy world vaguely connected to our own to which people could escape however they were cast in real life, and take on a character of their own making. McNeil writes: "Why on earth would I be myself online—a person I hated?"[2] A lot of teens logging on to the early social internet of the late 1990s and early 2000s shared this sentiment. Sadly, many teens *today* feel the same way without the same luxury of widespread anonymity.

For many, like an awkward middle school boy unsure of himself, the anonymous internet was an oasis in the middle of a desert. It was a place to explore the wonders and curiosities of the world in a costume, away from the social stressors of real life.

> The anonymous internet was an oasis in the middle of a desert.

Exploration

Along with anonymity, the prospect of vast exploration called out through the dial-up tones that flooded our computer rooms. The harsh "eeeeee-rrrrrrrrr-eee-rrr" was like the sound of a rocket engine launching us to a virtual space demanding to be explored. The internet was a vast fantasy world where you could don a character costume and explore the wonders of the world, connect with people who believed differently from you, and learn what the world was like far beyond the walls of your home and the bounds of your daily life.

The world was on the internet, and all it took to explore it was hogging the phone line and waiting a few minutes for each web page to load. You may never make it to Italy in real life, but you could discover anything you wanted to know about Italian culture and perhaps even chat with some actual Italians. It was like the virtual version of a secret hideout you shared with your friends in the woods behind your house, but instead of skipping rocks on a pond and catching frogs from your secret hideout, you were exploring the world . . . virtually.

Even more than just exploration, though, the earliest days of the social internet provided an opportunity to build community with others. Though the anonymity of the social internet has waned, and the shine of exploration may have worn off, the appeal of community that was present at the first remains now, and it's the strongest appeal of all.

Community

The social internet can provide a sense of belonging for anyone, regardless of whether they can find that sense of belonging off-line. That is what makes the internet so special for so many. It's what kept them coming back in the dial-up days of the 1990s, and it's what keeps them addicted now, thirty years later.

For a young person, the early appeal of community on the social internet was the ability to find others who were enduring similar life experiences. We could meet people who had not only the same interests but also the same fears and insecurities.

For those of us who were the first to have it in our most formative, teenage years, the internet was able to show us that the difficult, uncomfortable feelings we had were not unique to us. Other people—a community—were out there struggling with the same things. The earliest forms of community on the social internet served as a collective voice saying, "You're not alone in this," for an entire generation of teens. That's what drew so many of us to keep logging on years ago, before addictive algorithms came into play.

A form of that community is still keeping people connected to the internet today. We need affirmation. We need attention. We need community. Finding community online can be refreshing, even when we have a solid community of friends and family members around us in our off-line lives. However, when we don't find community and affirmation in our off-line lives, we scratch and claw to find community and affirmation online. This can have some negative consequences we will explore later.

In the early days of the social internet, different kinds of users were drawn online by different appeals. Some wanted to escape their difficult off-line lives, don an anonymous identity, and play a character on the internet. Others didn't care so much about assuming a new identity as they did about discovering the great frontier of information that was now at their fingertips for however long they wanted to click and explore. Almost everyone was logging on to experience community of some kind, even if they had a healthy community off-line. These major factors got us online in the first place, but what has kept us online? What keeps us coming back, clicking, searching, and connecting, even as many of us recognize and lament the negative effects it has on us?

What Keeps Us Coming Back
to the Social Internet?

After all these years, and plenty of cautionary tales about the negative effects of the social internet, we all continue to log on. Why? What makes Americans check their phones ninety-six times per day (or once every ten minutes)?[3]

Two primary factors keep us coming back to the social internet: (1) the fear of missing out and (2) addiction. Let's briefly (and I mean *briefly*) explore them.

We Can't Miss Out

The fear of missing out (FOMO) is old news at this point—the term was added to the *Oxford English Dictionary* all the way back in 2013. When it feels like everyone is always on social media, we feel like we can't log off either. What if we miss something important?

The fear of missing out is not unique to the social internet. The social internet just activates the fear much more frequently than life off-line does. We fear not being informed. We fear invisibility. Nicholas Carr writes of "young people" in his book *The Shallows*: "If they stop sending messages, they risk becoming invisible."[4] This is true for everyone, not just young people, but it is certainly more prevalent among the digital natives who have never known life without the internet.

For so many, to engage on social media is to exist. Many of us need to be acknowledged by other people (through likes, comments, shares, etc.) in order to be reminded of our own existence. Likewise, we feel the need to be present online in order not to miss out on what our friends and family members are doing. Unfortunately, we become so obsessed with not missing out on what is happening *online* that we miss out on what is happening *off-line*. We care so much about keeping up with those far from us that we damage the relationships of those closest to us.

> We become so obsessed with not missing out on what is happening *online* that we miss out on what is happening *off-line*.

We're Addicted

We also stay engaged on the social internet because we're plainly addicted to the feelings it provides, good and bad. Our addiction is a major factor in what keeps us logging on even when it isn't making us happy.

In his book *Irresistible: The Rise of Addictive Technology and the Business of Keeping Us Hooked*, Adam Alter shares about a 2013 study conducted by psychologist Catherine Steiner-Adair. The study examined the effects of parents' online addiction on their children. "My mom is almost always on the iPad at dinner," a seven-year-old named Colin told Steiner-Adair. "She's always 'just checking.'"[5] We're addicted to "just checking" because we fear missing out on the latest controversy, the newest family photo, or the most recent development in the apparently amazing lives of all of our friends.

In *Irresistible*, Alter lists six basic ingredients of behavioral addiction that have been adapted to our online experience: goals, feedback, progress, escalation, cliff-hangers, and social interaction.[6] These ingredients, when mixed together, make the social internet feel like a sort of competition or video game—a process known as "gamification." Goals give us something to pursue. Feedback gives us an idea of how people perceive us. Progress gives us the feeling of productivity and achievement. Escalation makes the game more challenging and, thus, more rewarding. Cliff-hangers give us a sense of anticipation and a hunger for more. Social interaction reminds us we're human. With all of these factors at play, it's no wonder we're addicted to the social internet, even if we're "just checking." We feel the need to live in a virtual world that often seems more vibrant and real than our off-line world. Living two lives that are similar but not identical understandably creates stress and, more than likely, contributes to the clear connection between social media use and increasing levels of anxiety. More on this later.

Nicholas Carr writes in *The Shallows*: "The Net's interactivity gives us powerful new tools for finding information, expressing ourselves, and conversing with others. It also turns us into lab rats constantly pressing levers to get tiny pellets of social or intellectual nourishment."[7] It's easy to bemoan our collective addiction to the social internet. It's sad. It's incredibly difficult to detox. But, as Carr indicates, we didn't just get addicted on our own. A rat in a behavioral modification experiment may be addicted to tiny pellets, but it isn't aware of how it became addicted. Likewise, many of us are addicted to the attention and affirmation we receive when we press the virtual levers on the social internet, but like the rat in the experiment, we don't know how we got here.

Our addiction to the social internet is ours to overcome, but it isn't totally our fault. The social internet is designed with addiction in mind. The systems are designed to enslave our eyes. We've been set up. We're being played.

> The social internet is designed with addiction in mind.

Our Brains Have Been Hacked

In a 2017 interview with Mike Allen of Axios, Sean Parker, the first president of Facebook and founder of Napster, unveiled the dirty truth about how social media platforms like Facebook manipulate our brains. He said:

> The thought process that went into building these applications, Facebook being the first of them, . . . was all about: How do we consume as much of your time and conscious attention as possible? And *that means that*

we need to sort of give you a little dopamine hit every once in a while, because someone liked or commented on a photo or a post or whatever. And that's going to get you to contribute more content, and that's going to get you . . . more likes and comments. It's a social-validation feedback loop . . . exactly the kind of thing that a hacker like myself would come up with, because *you're exploiting a vulnerability in human psychology.* The inventors, creators—it's me, it's Mark [Zuckerberg], it's Kevin Systrom on Instagram, it's all of these people—understood this consciously. And we did it anyway.[8] (emphasis added)

The social internet is designed to be addictive. It is not a neutral tool humans discovered and decided to use nonstop on their own. Since the start, and especially in the more recent iterations, the social internet has been designed with the intent to get people addicted. The people who create the social media apps and websites you use every day and compulsively check at the dinner table, before bed, and while sitting at stoplights *want you to become enslaved* to these platforms.

You and I are being played.

We are, as Carr says in *The Shallows*, like rats in a psychological experiment. We are being prompted and prodded and poked, told that life is happening all around us, and we'd better check in to see what everyone's doing with their lives, what everyone thinks about the pictures of our kids, because if we don't, we might miss out on something "important." Like a rat that gets a treat when it pushes a lever, we are rewarded with a little red notification bubble or delightful ding if we're obedient and open the app like we're told. We think we're choosing to "just check in." We aren't. Our behavior has been so modified, our brain has been so deeply "hacked," as Parker puts it, that we believe our social media addiction is normal behavior. We don't see it as a problem. It's just how things are now.

How does it work? How are we drawn into the addiction? We are manipulated by the algorithms at play on our favorite social media platforms. Let me explain how Facebook works, as an example.

The primary goal of Facebook is to make money. That's fair. It's the right of any company in a capitalist economy to do that. The primary way Facebook makes money is by selling ads. The way Facebook sells so many ads is by capturing the data and attention of more people than any other social media platform. So Facebook needs to keep people using the platform in order to keep the value of its ads high.

The question you might naturally ask is: "How does Facebook keep people on its platform?" Good question. Facebook has engineered the platform in a number of ways to keep people scrolling, but one rises above them all: *divisiveness*.

In 2018, an internal investigation at Facebook reported: "Our algorithms exploit the human brain's attraction to divisiveness."[9] The investigation also revealed that the Facebook algorithm is designed to deliver "more and more divisive content in an effort to gain user attention & increase time on the platform."[10] *Facebook's own investigation* reported that its algorithm—the secret mathematical equation developed to determine what you see when you open Facebook—is designed to serve you "more and more divisive content in an effort to gain user attention and increase time on the platform." The results of that study were presented internally at Facebook and shelved. They buried the research. No one outside Facebook knew about that presentation until *The Wall Street Journal* reported about it in the spring of 2020.

Facebook *knows* that the most reliable way to keep you scrolling is to make you mad. Divisive content leads to more engagement than unifying content. Is it any wonder Facebook's algorithm was engineered to stoke divisiveness?

> Facebook *knows* that the most reliable way to keep you scrolling is to make you mad. Divisive content leads to more engagement than unifying content.

This kind of strategy is advantageous to Facebook's business model but harmful to the wellness of its users—a trade Facebook has happily made throughout its existence.

This is but one example of how the social media platforms to which so many of us are addicted operate. The goals of these platforms go far beyond "connecting users for the greater good of mankind," as so many Silicon Valley mission statements often sound. It just so happens that "connecting users for the good of mankind" is incredibly lucrative, and the generation of massive amounts of revenue by "connecting users" often comes at the cost of "the good of mankind." The sad reality is that a lot of people are terrible and wicked, and when you connect billions of people to one another through something like social media, you've made it easier for evil people to connect with other evil people and for evil people to prey on well-meaning people. Unfortunately, the platforms that equip evil people for perpetual evil make a profit whether or not their users are using the tools for good or ill.

Are you uncomfortable yet? Have you begun to sense the toxicity of the water?

This is how the social internet operates. We are addicted to "just checking in" to platforms that are engineered to keep our attention at any expense to the wellness of its users. To that point: How is our addiction to the social internet affecting the rest of our lives? In part 2, we will consider five specific ways the social internet shapes us. First, let's examine the general effects our addiction has wrought onto our lives.

CHAPTER 3

How Does the Social Internet Affect Our Lives?

Social media is like a drug" is a common analogy, but it's not as accurate as it could be.

The broader social internet and the various social media platforms within it are probably best understood as a drug *dealer*, dispensing a variety of narcotics, depending on the day, all of which hook us and make us feel unlike ourselves. Sometimes the content dealt by social media makes us feel great. Sometimes it makes us feel inadequate. Sometimes it energizes us. Sometimes it depresses us. Unfortunately, many of us are so used to these "highs" that we don't even recognize them as highs anymore—they're just normal. Or we recognize that something's off-kilter, but we don't think to connect it to our dependence on the kinds of content provided by our digital drug dealer.

The social internet is fundamentally changing how we live in ways far beyond what we do when we are online. The highs we get from our social internet addictions affect us beyond when we're using our preferred drug. As with any addiction, the effects of our enslavement spill out from the addiction itself into many facets of our lives.

Part 2 of this book, which follows this chapter, is devoted to five prevalent ways we are shaped by our relationship with and addiction to the social internet. But before we dive into those specifics, we ought to take a moment to observe, from a sort of thirty-thousand-foot view, the wide array of ways our lives are being altered by our social internet addiction.

We Are Polarized

The conversation around Americans, polarization, and the possibility that social media has worsened that polarization is not new. Psychologists, sociologists, and social media professionals often debate the extent to which social media has driven polarization. The 2016 United States presidential election was perhaps the pinnacle of these discussions.

Some believe social media has been the primary driver of the deep polarization pervading our country the last five to ten years, while others admit it is a factor but not a primary one. I align myself with the former viewpoint, that the social internet has been a primary driver of the deepening abyss between

Americans of differing political and ideological persuasions in the last decade. I think we can point to two primary pieces of evidence in support of this claim: (1) the social internet promotes tribalism, and (2) the social internet inhibits us from empathizing with others.

A Risk-Free, Cheap Tribalism

Tribalism is a basic human instinct. Since the earliest recordings of human history, there is evidence of one tribe of people attacking another tribe of people who live or think differently than they do. Groups of people who have the same values or worldviews often find one another, stick together, and attack those whom they view as a threat to their way of living. This is a basic human survival instinct, and it takes place in virtual spaces today as it has taken place in physical spaces for millennia.

In the early twentieth century, many scholars and philosophers, like media philosopher Marshall McLuhan who wrote the book *The Medium Is the Massage*, believed a technology would eventually come along that would establish a "global village," connecting the whole world. That technology, the internet, did come along. But the internet hasn't created a global village; it has provided an avenue for all the individual ideological villages of the world to fight with one another.

When our virtual tribes feel threatened, when another tribe with a different set of values or a competing worldview attempts to assert dominance over ours (or we think they're going to try), we spring to ready our defenses or even preemptively attack. Instead of defending a physical village against an opposing onslaught, we defend our virtual, ideological village from a virtual village with an opposing ideology. Even in the pre-internet twentieth century, tribal warfare wasn't as prevalent as it is today. Conflict has always existed, but the pervasiveness of the social internet has ignited a new penchant for tribalism. Why? Tribal conflict has become less risky and easier to manufacture.

The tribalism we see today is different from the tribalism of old and the tribalism of the pre-internet twentieth century. In the tribalism of old, you had to rally a large group of people who were willing to put their literal lives on the line in order to protect your village and everything you held dear. Plenty of people did it, but it was a significant ask—there was a lot at stake. In the pre-internet twentieth century, before the widespread use of the social internet, it was difficult for one ideological tribe to fight with another ideological tribe on a daily basis. Outside of talking heads debating the merits of their tribe on national TV, masses of people could not be in conflict about which political or ideological tribe was superior unless countries actually went to war with each other (as they did).

> Conflict has always existed, but the pervasiveness of the social internet has ignited a new penchant for tribalism.

Today, tribalism is much less risky than it was at the dawn of humanity and much easier than it was in the pre-internet twentieth century. Today, all it takes to defend your village from another village is some free time, an internet connection, and a fervor for what you believe is right. It doesn't require you to be willing to risk your life or be asked to represent your tribe on a national TV program. You can go to war right from your pocket whenever you want, with (seemingly) little consequence.

This fuels polarization. When you can always be at war, defending what you think is most important, with little consequence to your livelihood, why would you ever lay down your sword and make peace? Many feel they must always fight, for if they let down their guard for a moment, an enemy might seize cultural territory or influence.

Personalization Destroys Empathy

The second major factor that drives polarization on the social internet is that the personalization of our primary social media platforms makes it difficult for us to empathize and see why others believe what they do. Virtually every major part of the internet wants to customize your experience to be most suitable for you. Part of the reason websites want to personalize your experience is so they can better understand you and more effectively target ads at you. The other reason websites want to personalize your experience is because the more personally tailored your experience feels, the more likely you are to return to that website.

The way this plays out is most commonly seen in algorithms delivering you content with which you agree. The obvious problem with this is that such feedback loops or "filter bubbles" of content that reinforce what we believe about everything can lead us to believe no other views exist. That's not good. These filter bubbles, or "echo chambers" as they are often called, do not lead to conflict as much as once believed (more on that later), but they still do make it hard to empathize with other people.

The hyper-personalization of our internet experience hinders our ability to see why other people believe what they believe. On the face of it, filter bubbles and hyper-personalization seem problematic because they may entrench us in our own beliefs. But beyond that, the broader problem is that it is impossible to know what the world looks like for someone who disagrees with us. Jaron Lanier explains this well in *Ten Arguments for Deleting Your Social Media Accounts Right Now.*[1] Polarization and filter bubbles have existed longer than the internet. Cable news encourages such filter bubbles. But at least with cable news, you can flip over to a cable news channel that pushes an ideology in opposition to yours to see what those people are hearing. On social media you cannot do this.

If you are a hard-core Conservative, and your Facebook feed is full of hard-core Conservative articles and opinions, you can't flip over to "hard-core Liberal" Facebook to see what they're saying. If you often feel like you are living in a different world from the people with whom you disagree, *it's because you are.* Living in our own little ideological worlds is not a new problem, but it is amplified by social media because we have no simple opportunity to peek into the little worlds of people who hold opposing views.

A good bit of research has been conducted even in the last couple of years that shows "echo chambers" are not the primary reason social media contributes to polarization. At least two studies published in the *Proceedings of the National Academy of the Sciences* since 2019 explore the relationship between echo chambers and polarization. The gist of the findings is that echo chambers have a much subtler effect on polarization than once thought and could even work against polarization. However, one study published in that same journal in June 2021 highlights the real effect of echo chambers online: conflict with "out-groups."

In a study called "Out-Group Animosity Drives Engagement on Social Media," authors Steve Rathje, Jay J. Van Bavel, and Sander van der Linden investigate the performance of divisive content on social media.[2] What they found is that the most engaging content on social media is content posted by one political group about an opposing political group. This content is, obviously, overwhelmingly negative, but it gets *twice* as many shares and retweets as content about the group doing the posting. This means that, say, posts by Democrats criticizing Republicans get twice as much engagement posts by Democrats promoting liberal ideas. The same goes for Republicans.

Perhaps the most interesting conclusion from the study, though, comes when the authors engage with the new data about echo chambers and their limited effects on polarization. The authors write (emphasis added):

> Even if people are exposed to more cross-partisan content than expected . . . our findings suggest that opposing views on social media may be excessively negative about one's own side. This may help explain why exposure to opposing views on Twitter can actually increase political polarization. . . . Thus, *the severity of online echo chambers appears to be a less important issue than the kind of content that tends to surface at the top of one's feed*, since exposure to divisive in-party or out-party voices is unlikely to be productive.[3]

What drives polarization on social media is not as much echo chambers per se, as it is our unwavering will to fight. This goes back to the cheap, risk-free tribalism we explored before. The polarization problem on social media lies with the conflict-laden content we consume more than it does with a lack of exposure to diverse ideas.

We Are Gullible

Conspiracy theories are not new. Some of the most commonly held conspiracy theories today revolve around real-world events that took place decades ago—the assassination of John F. Kennedy and the moon landing. But it sure seems like there are more conspiracy theories popping up today than there have been previously. Unfortunately, there are not many historical studies on the prevalence of conspiracy theories, so it's hard to say whether more people believe in conspiracy theories today than have in the past. But, even without data, it is hard to deny the fact that conspiracy theories are getting more attention than they ever have, and the social internet has certainly played a part.

In their book *A Lot of People Are Saying: The New Conspiracism and the Assault on Democracy*, authors Nancy Rosenblum and Russell Muirhead write: "New communications technologies that eliminate traditional gatekeeping functions of the media create an opening. Conspiracy entrepreneurs seize on this opening. So do opportunistic politicians."[4] In the past you had to have a certain amount of credibility to reach thousands of people with your opinions. Today, because of the democratization of platforms, a social media influencer who has eighty thousand followers because of her fashion sense and interior decorating skill could decide, on a random Thursday afternoon, to promote the theory that the earth is flat, and no one can stop her. This was not possible before. If Oprah had spent some of her afternoon talk show toying with the idea that the American government caused 9/11, she would have been run off television. Today, a social media influencer with millions of followers can make such a claim without any such consequence.

When you combine the "democratization of platform" ingredient with the "we live in our own filter bubble" ingredient, you get a deadly combination. Real harm can be done when a particular ideological group starts tossing around conspiracy theories in their corner of the social internet because anyone can promote wild theories without recourse, and our personalized worlds prevent us from seeing opposing points of view. The social internet has made us gullible because we've built our own little worlds led by microcelebrities, or "influencers," and many of us will believe anything they say.

We Are Unhappy

A tremendous amount of research is being done on the relationship between social media use and mental health. Virtually none of the findings tell a hopeful story.

Without citing a dozen research projects, let me summarize the findings of many of the most common studies: spending time on social media increases envy,[5] leads to unrealistic expectations and comparisons,[6] and has generally negative effects on mental health.[7]

It doesn't take a PhD or reading a bunch of studies by people who have PhDs to recognize this phenomenon and make a guess at why spending time online makes us unhappy. One could suggest, even, that it is in the best interest of social media platforms to make us unhappy, never feeling like we're good enough. Jaron Lanier explains: "If ordinary people were to get all happy and satisfied, they might take a moment away from the obsession with social media numbers and go frolic in the flowers or even pay direct attention to each other. But if they're all on edge about whether they're popular enough, worried about whether the world is imploding, or furious at morons who are thrust into the middle of their connections with friends and families, then they dare not disengage. They are hooked because of provoked natural vigilance."[8]

Social media platforms need us to be happy on their platforms but not so happy that we are satisfied with life completely and log off indefinitely. The small dissatisfaction of seeing an opinion with which we disagree or a picture of someone's life we envy draws us back to check in yet again. This is why much of the content delivered to us by social media algorithms either aligns closely with our beliefs or is the exact opposite of what we believe. Social media algorithms are designed to make us feel to the point of action. Positively or negatively, they just want us to feel something so strongly that we act on our feelings.

A lot of us, on the flip side, log on to the social internet to find some sort of happiness because our lives are so miserable off-line. We seek even a small, fleeting illusion of happiness and affirmation from people on the internet because we can't find any in the world around us. We seek out a funny cat video because, sadly, it's the best part of our day.

> For some, the internet leads to unhappiness. For others, the internet provides a brief taste of happiness that, however fleeting, tastes sweeter than real life off-line.

For some, the internet leads to unhappiness. For others, the internet provides a brief taste of happiness that, however fleeting, tastes sweeter than real life off-line. For just about all of us, the internet is making us more anxious.

We Are Anxious

Our use of and addiction to the social internet is making us more anxious. Mountains of data have been collected in the last few years that point to a clear relationship between increased social media use and increased experiences of anxiety and depression.[9]

Perhaps the most dramatic example of the correlation between social media use and symptoms of anxiety and depression comes from the current teenagers who make up Gen Z, or "iGen" as they have been called by researcher and author Jean Twenge. Authors Jonathan Haidt and Greg Lukianoff cite one particularly troubling study in their book *The Coddling of the American Mind*. Research shows that, in the early 2000s, just more than one-in-ten girls aged twelve to seventeen had a "major depressive episode" in the previous year. But, by 2016, nearly one-in-five girls aged twelve to seventeen had a major depressive episode in the previous year. *The rate of major depressive episodes among adolescent girls nearly doubled in less than a decade.* Haidt and Lukianoff note that adolescent boys also experienced an increase in depressive episodes but not as dramatic as that of girls.[10]

Girls are more likely to become anxious or depressed because of increased social media use than boys because the root of anxiety and depression in girls tends to lie more in social dynamics than it does for boys. Whereas boys often deal with social conflict through direct, physical confrontation, girls are more likely to deal with social conflict in ways exacerbated by social media, which is one explanation for their increased anxiety and depression.

In fact, since we're talking about the effects of increased social media use on teenagers, let's all go back to high school for a minute and bask in the aroma of Axe body spray and lunch room pizza.

Do you remember how it felt to walk the hallways of high school between classes or sit at the lunch table? Hallways and lunchrooms are the primary stages for social engagement in high school. Sure, you talk with your peers in class, but most of the time you're paying attention to lectures or doing work. Social dynamics are most active between classes or while eating lunch.

Everyone, even the kids who say they aren't, is performing in some way. High school hallways and lunchrooms are like little stages on which teenagers craft their personas and identities among their peers. It's exciting and stressful, just like performing on any stage. In the twentieth century teenagers left these social stages when they went home. Unless they had plans to attend a social function in the evening or hit the mall, the social dynamics of high school were left for phone calls with trusted friends until the next school day.

Today, as Derek Thompson says in his book *Hit Makers*, teenagers are always in the high school hallways.[11] There is no escaping the social stages on which teenagers perform because instead of walking the runway of the high school hallways for a couple of hours a day, five days a week, teenagers have their personal stages in their pockets, calling them to perform every hour of every day with no opportunity to retreat to a social backstage for rest from their ever-present performance.

Is there any wonder, then, why teenagers are more anxious and depressed than before? If you remember the social stressors of the high school hallways and lunchrooms, you can empathize with the feelings today's teens have as they carry those performance arenas around in their pockets all the time.

Bo Burnham is a comedian, actor, and director. His career began when he started posting off-color comedic songs to a YouTube channel when he was in high school and YouTube was a relatively new platform. Burnham and I are roughly the same age, and I remember watching his videos in high school, ashamed at how hard I was laughing because of how inappropriate they were (and are). Burnham's 2021 Netflix special *Inside* is a comedy and a tragedy all wrapped into one hour-long program, and I could write pages about it here, as it is full of masterful commentary on the absurdity of the social internet. But instead, I want to call attention to a quote he gave when he was interviewed following the release of a movie he wrote and directed, *Eighth Grade*.[12]

The movie, which accurately depicts the most awkward aspects of the modern eighth-grade experience, naturally features social media heavily. The film's main character is an aspiring YouTuber, much like Burnham was when he was in high school. Burnham says regarding the social pressures young people face today that no one has ever had to face before:

> What is the feeling of walking through your life and not just living your life, not just living your life—which is already [hard] and impossible—but also taking inventory of your life, being a viewer of your own life, living an experience and at the same time hovering behind yourself and watching yourself live that experience? Being nostalgic for moments that haven't happened yet. Planning your future to look back on it.
>
> Those are really weird, dissociative things that are, I think, new because of the specific structure of social media and how it disassociates ourselves from ourselves.[13]

We find ourselves in a spot in which we feel we have to live our lives and create a documentary of our lives at the same time. We, as Burnham says, hover behind ourselves and watch ourselves live our lives *while living our lives*. Is it any wonder mental health crises are on the rise?

Another unfortunate reality is that this is not limited to teenagers. Data shows that social media use is adversely affecting the mental health of adults just as it is with teens. Sure, it's safe to say adults may feel less peer pressure to be as active on social media as teens are, but we're all performing in the same way. With constant performance comes constant pressure. With constant pressure comes the gnawing anxiety that you're going to fail in the spotlight at some point. How long can you perform before you need to take a break? What if you feel like you can never take a break and log off?

The Social Internet Is Changing Us

An entire book could be written about just the contents of this chapter. The purpose of this chapter is to briefly explore a few primary ways in which our extended, increased participation in the social internet has changed us over time. I feel a bit guilty not diving into each of these points or citing every study I've come across on social media and anxiety or social media and happiness because these are important aspects of our relationship with the social internet. But you can seek out those studies yourself and the books that explore them in more depth. If you need a place to start, begin with the ones I've cited throughout the chapter.

What I hope you have seen is this: the social internet is changing us and mostly in negative

> With constant performance comes constant pressure. With constant pressure comes the gnawing anxiety that you're going to fail in the spotlight.

ways. The social internet incentivizes us to huddle close to our tribes and lash out at those who are different. In defense of our tribes, we are often gullible, willing to believe whatever will preserve the perceived good of the tribe and take ground from those with whom we disagree. We seek out happiness and fulfillment through the social internet because we fail to find it in our real, off-line lives. We live in a perpetual state of anxiety, wondering if we're being judged by what we share online, in fear of what would happen if we stopped posting altogether. Would we be completely forgotten? No longer exist?

PART 2

Five Ways the Social Internet Shapes Us

CHAPTER 4

We Believe Attention Assigns Value

One of the most pervasive lies we believe when we engage with the social internet is that the more attention someone or something gets, the more valuable that popular person or content is.

What does that mean? That one lie is really best understood as two separate but related lies: (1) a trending or viral piece of content is inherently important simply because it's popular; and (2) when people pay attention to me, they're telling me I'm valuable. The overarching lie is rooted in the belief that attention equals value—that what is *most popular* is *most valuable.*

When it comes to what "trends" on any part of the internet, we have come to believe if it is trending, it is important, and we ought to give it our attention, no matter how insignificant or downright foolish it may seem. Likewise, we have come to believe that how much attention we receive is an accurate measure of how important or valuable we are. We take pride in our followers, the number of likes we receive, and how many people retweet our ideas.

Psychological Science is widely considered to be one of the best peer-reviewed academic journals in the field of psychology and social sciences. The abstract of a 2016 article on the effects of peer influence and social media on the human brain summarizes the findings of the study, saying, "Viewing photos with many (compared with few) likes was associated with greater activity in neural regions implicated in reward processing, social cognition, imitation, and attention."[1] Like the snowball cliché, content that attracts attention is deemed valuable; therefore it gets more attention, appears more valuable, attracts more attention, and grows in perceived "value." This sort of attention and affirmation feeds a loop that plays into our engineered addiction to the social internet.

If we're going to be honest, the false belief that attention equals value isn't a new phenomenon. The most popular kids in school have always been the ones who get the most attention—after all, *getting attention* is sort of the definition of popularity. Attention does equal popularity, on- and off-line. Because so many of us wrongly find our value in how popular we are, it follows that if attention equals popularity, and popularity equals importance/value, then attention equals importance/value. This is not true, but believing it can lead to some real, deep mental, emotional, and spiritual issues.

The social internet is a stage on which we perform and receive attention and affirmation from people around the world. Riding the attention and affirmation of a social media audience can lead to piles of money and worldwide fame, like in the case of influencers, or it can lead to depression and anxiety, eventuating in self-harm, as in the case of an increasing number of people. Often, it even leads to both. An influencer who lives by the fickle fancies of internet stardom also suffers the consequences of unhappy fans. For the countless people addicted to social media, it is nearly impossible to retreat to a backstage and find relief from the pressures of performing. When we live our lives online, we are constantly on stage, reaching for a sense of fulfillment we believe can be achieved if we just get enough attention.

The reason we believe the lie that attention determines value or worth is because there is actually a shade of truth to that idea in the economy that undergirds the social internet. When it comes to internet advertising, attention is the most valuable resource there is. This is the kernel of truth to the idea. Attention is incredibly valuable in terms of dollars and cents for advertisers and the owners of the social media platforms that demand our attention. At the same time, attention does not determine the value of a person, event, or topic. As Christians, we are to find our identity in the finished work of Christ and our standing as image bearers of God. Even for non-Christians, personal value or purpose shouldn't be sought in the attention given by others. Such a pursuit leads to all kinds of emotional and spiritual distress.

Mark Zuckerberg, Kevin Systrom, and others are wealthy because they applied their computer science skills to hijack the human brain and sell attention for a big profit. First, they figured out that a human will check a screen hundreds or thousands of times per day in order to be affirmed, engaging the pleasure centers of the brain—like a dog ringing a bell to get a treat. Then, especially once the screens moved from desks to pockets, they figured out how to sell space on those pocket-sized screens for billions of dollars. We live in a confusing reality in which attention is monetarily valuable to the companies that sell our attention, but it cannot fill the value void we feel in our hearts, no matter how hard we try to fill it. Let's go back in time, to the 1990s, to see how this began.

AOL and the Attention Economy

It is often said that "data is the new oil." If data is the new oil, *attention is the oil rig.*

User data is what social internet companies use to make money. But in order for social internet companies to get our data, they need our attention. Attention is the means by which social internet companies harvest our data. Our attention is the oil rig; our data is the oil.

In 2019, Facebook reported that it made about $70 billion on advertising revenue. How on earth is a social media company able to make almost double the annual revenue of Coca-Cola on advertising alone? Our attention. How much is our collective attention to Facebook worth? In 2019 it was worth $70 billion. In 2020, it was over $84 billion. Harvesting attention makes Facebook financially wealthy and leaves us spiritually impoverished.

The social internet was in its nascent stages in the 1990s, and it was revolutionized by America Online (AOL). We already explored a bit of AOL's impact on the evolution of the social internet in chapter 2, so we won't rehash all of that here. But I do think it would be helpful for us to explore how AOL demonstrated that the *social* aspect of the internet is what is most likely to grab the attention of internet users.

All of the companies and services that were jockeying for position in the early days of the social internet were obsessed with the features of the services they provided. Prodigy recognized much of what would make the internet revolutionize the world: online shopping and hyper-targeted advertising based on data collected from users. CompuServe sort of branded itself as the internet service for tech-savvy users—the dominant demographic for a brief time when home internet first began to expand in influence. Two primary factors made AOL stand out: (1) it targeted the masses, and (2) it focused on the social aspect of the internet.

AOL recognized, sort of by accident, that what most kept people's attention on their platform was their interactions with other people—not flashy services like shopping or multimedia. AOL came to dominate the earliest days of home internet because they mailed millions of trial discs to Americans to see what their service was all about and because they focused on making it easy for people to connect with other people, even if they had never used a personal computer before.

Tim Wu writes in his book *The Attention Merchants*: "The strategy of using people to gain the attention of other people was in retrospect inspired, even if arrived at more or less by accident."[2] How was it an "accident" that AOL stumbled into the realization that the social aspect of the internet is the most valuable? Because at the time it was so tempting for these internet companies to get wrapped up in the features of their service and what made their service special, and AOL lucked into having headline features (email and chat) that were more about connecting people to people than people to information. What made the internet special in the eyes of its users was the ability to connect with others. It just so happened that AOL, of all the internet services at the time, was designed to do that most effectively, and when they mailed trial discs to millions of Americans, they built the world's largest social network—long before anyone was talking about any of the social media companies we use today.

To make a long story short, AOL eventually began trying to capitalize on all of the attention it had—even going as far as selling the names and addresses of its users to direct-mail companies![3] They had the right idea—that monetizing attention and user data was the future of the social internet—but they didn't execute it as effectively as social internet companies today do, and eventually, it led (along with a number of other factors) to the shuttering of the platform.

But before AOL imploded, it had a profound effect on the future of the internet. It showed innovators, investors, and users that the most financially valuable aspect of the internet is the ability to interact with other people. When internet users demonstrated that connecting with other people is the most important part of the internet to them, innovators and investors capitalized.

If socializing is the most valuable part of the internet for users, it's the most lucrative part for businesses. Where there is a lot of attention, there is a lot of money to be made.

> Where there is a lot of attention, there is a lot of money to be made.

How much money, exactly? Here are the ad revenues of three of the major social internet companies from 2020:

- Google: about $146.9 billion
- Facebook: about $84.2 billion
- Twitter: about $3.7 billion

The collective attention of the social internet has a tremendous amount of value when it comes to advertising revenue. Major corporations like Coca-Cola, Starbucks, and so many others are transferring unprecedented sums of money to companies like Twitter and Google to get their stuff in front of your face. They're willing to spend more money than you'll ever see in your lifetime to get something, really *anything*, to "go viral." Why? Because they recognize what a lot of us haven't: *when something gets a lot of attention, we assign it a disproportionate amount of value.*

We believe that the pinnacle of the internet experience, and perhaps the pinnacle of life itself, is being noticed and going viral. This is a problem.

Attention and Our Social Economy

In 2015, I was folding laundry in the bedroom of our Nashville apartment one evening when I came across one of the most disturbing podcast episodes I had ever heard. Ira Glass began episode 573 of *This American Life*, titled "Status Update," by interviewing Julia (thirteen years old), Jane (fourteen), and Ella (fourteen) about how they use Instagram and how it affects their lives.[4]

The teenage girls come to the studio, Glass says, and take pictures of themselves, like they do anytime they're someplace together. The girls take their pictures, post them to Instagram, and Glass begins talking with them about what is supposed to happen now. A big measurement of success for an Instagram post in the mind of a teenage girl is how many likes it receives in the first minute. Ella says two likes in the first minute is typical. The girls are impressed when the picture Ella posted gets six likes in the first minute—at eleven o'clock in the morning on a day with no school, which is not prime time.

The girls, who just started high school in 2015 (and are now likely in college), talk about how commenting something like, "OMG You're so pretty," on the photo of someone they barely know is basically saying, "I want to be friends with you." Everyone does it they say. It's how teenage girls affirm one another. Approaching a potential friend in the hallway at school or in the lunchroom may appear desperate and needy. Instead, the girls comment, "You're so cute I hate you," on a selfie to say the same, which is more socially appropriate.

The process of posting a selfie and commenting, "OMG You're so pretty!" or something similar while they wait for the same kinds of comments on their posts is "mindless," as Ella, one of the girls, says. Glass catches that and asks: "It's mindless. And so since it's mindless, does it still work? Does it make you feel good?" All of the girls say that yes, it does make them feel good, even though they know they do it mindlessly, and the people commenting on their selfies do the same. Mindless affirmation makes us feel good because we have come to believe that attention determines value.

As Glass continues to talk to the girls about Instagram, how they use it, and what certain kinds of comments mean, a clear trend emerges: attention is social currency. Even worse, attention is a drug. As I wrote before, this isn't new. Attention and social status were related before the social internet jumped into our pockets, but it's never been like this. We have been conditioned to believe, by the systems that undergird the social internet, that one of the primary ways someone can tell us they care about us is by interacting with the online version of ourselves.

In 2004, when Facebook was first making its way to college campuses beyond Harvard, a student journalist at *The*

Stanford Daily wrote, "Nothing validates your social existence like the knowledge that someone else has approved you or is asking for your permission to list them as a friend. It's bonding and flattering at the same time."[5] We've always craved attention and affection—the human desire for approval is not a new desire—but we've never had such immediate and constant access to it.

We've become addicted to attention, literally. We're addicted to the dopamine that runs through our brains when we are paid attention. We aren't blameless in this tragedy, but we didn't become addicted to attention on our own. We had help.

Attention Is the Ultimate High of Social Media Addiction

As Sean Parker, the first president of Facebook, said in his interview with Axios about how they designed Facebook, "We need to give you a little dopamine hit every once in a while." When we open up our phones and see the little red badges pinned to the corners of the apps to which we are enslaved, we instinctively wonder, "Who commented on what? Did someone message me? How many likes do I have now?"

We give our attention to these virtual vending machines of hollow affirmation because it's often easier than paying attention to real life. To mix a couple of metaphors that have been in play throughout this chapter: attention is a currency and a drug. Getting attention is the ultimate high of our addiction to the social internet, alongside getting affirmation, which is really just the positive subset of attention. Ultimately, many of us find ourselves thinking like this, even though most of us would never verbalize it:

> My one-year-old daughter doesn't tell me she thinks my blog post was profound. She just throws food on the floor and poops in the bathtub.
>
> My dog doesn't listen to my podcast. He just constantly rings the bells at the back door, demanding I take him outside.
>
> My pastor doesn't like any of my selfies. He just calls me out for not coming to church.
>
> Why would I pay more attention to my daughter, my dog, or my pastor, when I can just post more stuff online for people to like, comment, and share?

Deep down, many of us want to be famous. Not necessarily because we think we can be rich and famous around the world, but primarily because to be famous is to be paid attention, and to be paid attention is to be recognized as valuable, which we feel we lack.

The vast stores of attention now being given to people on the internet offer a sort of gold rush on fame. It feels like anyone can become famous, even a mom with a Chewbacca mask in the Kohl's parking lot. Tim Wu, toward the end of

The Attention Merchants, reflects on what the early days of the attention economy ultimately wrought. He writes: "In actuality, fame, or the hunger for it, would become something of a pandemic, swallowing up more and more people and leaving them with the scars of chronic attention-whoredom."[6]

Many of us are addicted to the social internet because we are addicted to attention and affirmation. We seek to be attention rich because we are joy poor. In our sin, we believe we are to be the hero and center of our lives, and if we play the social internet game correctly, we can find the attention and affirmation online that we so desperately long for off-line.

> To be paid attention is to be recognized as valuable, which we feel we lack.

If you're a Christian reading this, be reminded that you are God's workmanship, created in Christ to do good works (Eph. 2:10), and that you have been raised with Christ (Col. 3:1). Your value is not determined by how much attention you do or do not receive. You are loved by God as his image bearer (Gen. 1:27) and as his child (John 1:12).

Now that we have focused on the attraction of attention, let's explore what we give up when we give our attention to the companies behind the social internet. Yielding our attention costs us something.

CHAPTER 5

We Trade Our Privacy
for Expression

I t is often said, "If the product/website/app/etc. you're using is free, *you are the product*." That sounds terrifyingly dehumanizing, doesn't it? But it's not true.

The reality is actually even worse.

We aren't even the product. Big social internet companies don't care about *us*. It's our *data* they want. *Our data* is the product.

How do they get our data? By harvesting our attention. The collective attention of all of us, the users of the social internet, is driving the trillion-dollar attention economy of the most lucrative companies in the world. To use the metaphor from the last chapter: our attention is the oil rig, and our data is the oil, tapped out of our brains by way of keeping our attention.

When the attention economy started, the goal was to learn as much about user behavior as possible so that advertisements could be placed in front of the most interested eyes. Today, the goal of the attention economy is not just to learn about human behavior but to *influence* or, often more maliciously, to *manipulate* human behavior.

Why are we talking about this in a book about our relationship with the social internet? I think it's pretty clear. Every major social internet platform you and I use on a daily basis is available to us free of charge. We don't have to pay per Google search. Facebook and Instagram don't charge a monthly fee. What we don't realize is that we are paying for these services, just not with money. We're paying with our data. We're paying with our privacy. None of us read the "Terms and Conditions" or "Terms of Service" on the websites or apps we use, so we don't know what we're giving up by using them. In this chapter, I want to show you that social media may be free of charge, but it still comes at a great cost to our privacy.

> Social media may be free of charge, but it still comes at a great cost to our privacy.

Why Should I Care about My Data and Privacy?

Before we continue, I want to address a question you're likely asking: "Why should I care about my data and privacy?"

One of my good friends, Jonathan, often says to me, "They (whoever 'they' are—I'm not sure) have everything already. It doesn't matter if I give them access to my data." This is the most common view of people I talk with about our data and privacy being thrown into jeopardy by the social internet and the attention economy in general.

Another common sentiment is: "Why should I care about privacy? I have nothing to hide." I totally understand the sentiment, but I don't think it's actually true. Your family knows what you do when you go into the bathroom, but you still shut the door! You aren't trying to hide anything there either!

Secrecy and privacy aren't the same. We ought to care about what happens to our data. We ought to want to protect our privacy—however impossible doing so may seem—because without privacy we have no shield against malicious people who may want to use our data against us. And often those malicious people aren't shadowy foreign governments but the social internet companies themselves, or other people who use them.

My friend gave birth to twin boys a few years ago. The boys were born prematurely, and she chronicled their journey through the NICU on her Instagram so that friends and family could keep up with their progress and pray for them. Eventually, my friend was alerted to a woman who set up an Instagram account and used the pictures of my friend's children, claiming they were her own, to ask for money to pay hospital bills and such. This is a horrifying story, but you can find many similar, even worse, experiences if you look around online. My friend didn't do anything wrong. She simply used social media the way it's meant to be used. She didn't have anything to hide. She just wanted to share about her boys' growth and health. But neither you nor I would want what happened to my friend to happen to us.

Privacy matters. We willingly give up some sense of privacy when we post to social media. We express ourselves or post pictures of our lives to social media with the understanding that friends and family will be able to keep up with us and stay in touch. What we often don't think about is the hidden costs of such expression. We don't think about a real person using our content to impersonate us or blackmail us. We don't think about the possibility that a social media platform is selling our data to other companies so they can manipulate us to buy their stuff or vote a certain way.

Is self-expression worth the cost of our privacy? You may think it is, and that's okay. But I want to make sure you are aware of the price you're paying when you click the checkbox on the Terms of Service. We are all paying a price, even if it isn't hitting our bank accounts.

> Is self-expression worth the cost of our privacy?

Behavioral Surplus and Modification

Shoshana Zuboff's tome *The Age of Surveillance Capitalism* dives into the data-for-profit reality and the consequences of the attention economy. "Surveillance capitalism," defined by

Zuboff, "unilaterally claims human experience as free raw material for translation into behavioral data."[1] Who participates in surveillance capitalism? Most internet companies you know, but Facebook and Google are two of the most prominent players. We will explore them in more depth later.

The big problem with surveillance capitalism, according to Zuboff, is that it is built on the manipulation of people for the benefit of others. She writes: "Surveillance capitalists know everything *about us*, whereas their operations are designed to be unknowable *to us*. They accumulate vast domains of new knowledge *from us*, but not *for us*. They predict our futures for the sake of others' gain, not ours."[2] We ought to be concerned with surveillance capitalism because it begins with internet users like you and me sharing information about our lives, and it ends with large companies, or even governments, using that information we share for profit, surveillance, or worse—and we get nothing out of the deal except for the sweet satisfaction of personal expression, and the occasional spookily accurate ad for the moisturizing hand soap we were just talking about with our spouse.

At the core of surveillance capitalism is the most valuable resource available in the world today: behavioral surplus. What is behavioral surplus? Simply put, behavioral surplus is the data we intentionally and unintentionally deposit into the social internet in everything we do. It is often characterized as "data exhaust," like the leftover information that expels itself as we engage online. Behavioral surplus is how you word a sentence in a Google search. It's where your iPhone says you are at any given moment. It's your smart thermostat recognizing the temperature you prefer when you go to bed. It's Instagram recognizing that you like pictures of dogs more than cats. Behavioral surplus is all of the little signals we give internet companies about who we are, where we live, what we care about, and what makes us tick—data that goes far beyond the status updates we actively type into these platforms.

In the early days of the social internet, Google recognized how much it could learn about its users from their searches. Google was picking up data from users not just by the actual words they typed but through all kinds of other data bread crumbs they dropped along the way. Google, and eventually other companies, soon figured out they could use this user information to make a massive profit. This data didn't cost Google anything, but it was incredibly valuable to advertisers.

It was the leftover data beyond the search—hence the term "data exhaust"—that proved most lucrative. The exhaust dispelled from our earliest Google searches was captured and sold to advertisers who wanted to get their ads in front of relevant audiences. This discovery, that data bread crumbs from users could be harvested and sold, was pioneered by Google and led to much of the social internet surveillance activity we see today. But, in the early days, social internet companies were primarily concerned with harvesting data and selling access to it for advertisers to be able to place hyper-targeted ads. Today that method still exists, but the primary goal has shifted from harvesting as much behavioral surplus as possible to weaponizing that behavioral surplus for behavioral modification or manipulation.

Zuboff talked with a number of engineers and data scientists about what their apps, programs, and websites are designed to do as they collect data about user behavior. One chief data scientist at a well-respected Silicon Valley education company said: "The goal of everything we do is to change people's actual behavior at scale. We want to figure out the construction of changing a person's behavior, and then we want to change how lots of people are making their day-to-day decisions. . . . We can test how actionable our cues are for them and how profitable certain behaviors are for us."[3]

That data scientist was just one of a handful who made similar comments.

So, to summarize briefly: most of the social internet apps and websites you use primarily exist to gather and monetize your data. Further, they are actively looking for ways to manipulate you into making decisions that make them more money. We, the users, are nothing more than rich data deposits from which these companies can extract the most valuable resource in the world: *information about who we are and how we like to spend our money.*

We are not the product. It's worse than that. The data points that numerically represent our lives are the product. We are just the wells that are tapped for the data. To these companies, our hopes, dreams, and personalities are all window dressing that get in the way of the actions we take online.

Google pioneered surveillance capitalism with its discovery and weaponization of behavioral surplus, and it continues to do so. But Facebook stood on the shoulders of Google's initial discovery, and it has figured out the most grotesque ways to suck the data out of its users and manipulate them to dance as it pleases. Let's dive into that darkness.

How Facebook Manipulates You for a Profit

I have to say up front that Facebook is far from the only social internet company that participates in the surveillance capitalist process of harvesting our data in order to use it for behavioral modification and a profit. Google pioneered this industry, as I said before. Instagram is owned by Facebook, so obviously it participates. Twitter participates to some extent, though it is not nearly as invasive in its data collection as the other platforms. Amazon does this but isn't traditionally considered part of the social internet. Though not a social internet company, Apple is one of the most trustworthy companies in this regard. It values data privacy as a human right and takes active measures to protect Apple users from many of the practices we're exploring in this chapter. This is why, as an example, I could never recommend someone use Alexa, but I use Siri with some frequency. There is a difference, and that difference is a philosophical understanding of privacy as a human right (Apple) or privacy as an obstacle to billions in revenue (Amazon, Google, etc.).

Facebook and its suite of platforms (Instagram, WhatsApp, etc.) have more users than any other social internet platform. In 2020, Facebook alone was averaging about 2.5 billion monthly active users. That's roughly a third of the world's population. So, given that Facebook is playing a manipulative role in the lives of a third of the world's population, we need to pick on them before anyone else.

Before we get into the particular ways in which Facebook harvests the data of its users to manipulate them, I should explain the basic reason Facebook exists. A third of the world uses Facebook on a regular basis, and most of us probably don't think about the platform itself. Most of us just think about the content we see on Facebook. The platform itself, in our eyes, is just a host for funny videos, inspiring quotes, controversial opinions, or pictures of loved ones.

But Facebook's number one goal is not just to deliver you content you want to see. In order to understand why and how Facebook harvests user data for behavioral modification and manipulation, we have to recognize that Facebook's ultimate goal goes beyond showing you content you want to see. The ultimate goal of Facebook runs deeper than that.

Let's reverse engineer how Facebook works, beginning with their end goal and then working back to what you and I see when we open the app.

- Facebook ultimately exists to make money.
- Facebook makes most of its money by selling advertisements.

- Facebook sells targeted advertisements by keeping our attention and harvesting our data.

- Facebook keeps our attention and harvests our data by delivering us interesting content that makes us engage and stay on Facebook.

The primary goal of Facebook is to make money. That's fair. There is nothing wrong with that.

How does Facebook make money? Facebook makes money by selling billions of dollars in ads.

How does Facebook sell ads so effectively? By harvesting our data and keeping our attention.

How does Facebook harvest our data and keep our attention? By encouraging us to share what is going on in our lives, by following us around the internet, and by delivering us content they know will drive us to act in some way.

Do you see how that works? Most of us just think of Facebook as an online platform where we can share what's going on in our lives, see what's going on in others' lives, and watch some funny or heartwarming videos. But that is really just the surface of what Facebook is doing. All of the ways we use Facebook—every click, every video view, every pause to read a meme—is harvested and used to monitor and eventually modify our behavior—usually just for profit, but this data has been used by third parties for more nefarious goals. Let's review the three basic ways Facebook collects and uses our data: our personal expression, our internet activity, and our content consumption.

Our Personal Expression

Facebook reads everything you post to Facebook. I don't mean there's some software engineer in Silicon Valley scrolling through your profile—that would be too expensive. Facebook's artificial intelligence collects data points about you based on what you put into the platform. Do you have your current city of residence in your profile? Facebook has that. Maybe you told Facebook your anniversary is June 1? They have that too. But it goes far beyond just what's in your profile. Did you post a status update asking about the best tires for your 2017 Honda Odyssey minivan? Facebook now knows you have a 2017 Honda Odyssey minivan. Did you post about your recent bout with anxiety and depression? Facebook now knows you have mental health issues.

Our desire for personal expression is the gasoline that keeps the social internet running. We want people to know who we are and what is going on in our lives. As we share all of this information, we are put into categories—a minivan owner with anxiety whose anniversary is June 1—and Facebook delivers us advertising based on this data. This means that, theoretically, someone who works for a tire company could run ads targeting minivan owners with anxiety saying something like, "Afraid your tires are unsafe? Buy your tires from us before you regret it!"

Facebook makes $80+ billion a year in advertising because their ads can be specifically targeted to a particular audience in a way television or radio ads never could. In the 1990s, a car company could have theorized, "A lot of moms watch *Oprah*, so let's run a minivan ad during *Oprah*," but they couldn't know for sure if those moms already had a minivan or were maybe in the market for one. Today, a car company could run that same ad on Facebook targeting twenty- to twenty-nine-year-old mothers who have children ages birth to two, do not own a minivan already, but have been searching for different minivans online. The Facebook ad is more accurate, more likely to drive a sale, and thus, more valuable.

Facebook uses everything we put into its platform to place us in virtual buckets or categories that make advertisers' ads much more effective. Facebook says they harvest our data and deliver us relevant ads because relevant ads make the user experience more enjoyable. If you attempt to turn off the ability for other websites to tell Facebook about a recent purchase or other activity, Facebook warns you that your ads may not be as "relevant" or "personalized."

Which would you prefer: Facebook ads for baby clothes misinterpreted as relevant for you based on your recent post about your miscarriage (which is real and happens), or Facebook ads for organic cat food based on zero data about your web activity whatsoever? I'll take the cat food, thank you. But that does lead us to the second way Facebook harvests data to use for profit: our internet activity *away* from Facebook.

Our Internet Activity

Allow me to introduce you to the Facebook Pixel—a small piece of code installed in countless websites that sends your web activity back to Facebook to give them more information about you. The Facebook Pixel is why you see advertisements for workout apparel after buying a new pair of running shoes. It's why you see an advertisement for Tylenol after searching, "Is my headache a sign of stress or a brain tumor?" No one knows how many websites on the internet have the Facebook Pixel installed. . . . Well, except probably Facebook, but like most of their data, they don't make that public. The number is likely in the tens of millions. It is safe to say it is on most every shopping website we use, though, and it is Facebook's mechanism tracking our every move across the internet.

Why does Facebook care what we do on Amazon or any other website? You guessed it: to harvest and monetize our data. On the Facebook platform, Facebook is gathering the data we give it. It's placing us in different buckets or categories so advertisers can be sure to target their ads exactly where they want them. The Facebook Pixel allows them to gather more data on us beyond the virtual walls of Facebook. Companies install the Facebook Pixel on their websites to collect data about audiences so they can target them again later.

Did you go to your favorite online retailer and fill a cart with products but not buy them? You will likely see a Facebook ad for those products soon. How? The Facebook Pixel connected your shopping cart to your Facebook account.

In the "Settings & Privacy" section of the Facebook settings, you can turn off Facebook's ability to track you around the web, though they will warn you that your ads will be less personalized. Here's the problem though: there's really no way to know if Facebook *does* stop tracking you around the web. It's sort of like the "walk" button we all push at a crosswalk—we press it, hoping it will work with no real idea if it does.

Facebook has routinely, throughout its history, made "mistakes" that happen to work in the favor of its customers (advertisers) and to the detriment of its users (you and me). If, someday, Facebook has to admit, "Whoops! The ability to turn off web activity tracking didn't work! Sorry, it should work now," I would not be surprised in the slightest. Facebook harvests our data from how we express ourselves on Facebook and based on the actions we take on millions of other websites. It doesn't end there. Back on the Facebook platform, Facebook collects data based not only on what we post but also on what we consume.

> Facebook has routinely, throughout its history, made "mistakes" that happen to work in the favor of its customers (advertisers) and to the detriment of its users (you and me).

Our Content Consumption

The third common way Facebook harvests data from us is by learning who we are through the kind of content we consume. In the marketing world, "engagement" is the most important metric to measure social media effectiveness. A number of actions are considered engagement: liking, commenting, sharing, watching a video, pausing while scrolling to view a picture, and more. All of those actions are kinds of engagement that Facebook (and other platforms) uses to track what keeps our attention. If you watch a few funny videos on Facebook, Facebook sees your watch time and is more likely to deliver you funny videos in the future. If you comment on a bunch of political articles, Facebook sees that political articles drive you to action, and it will likely deliver you a lot more political articles in the future.

Facebook is constantly learning what keeps our attention and drives us to action so it can keep feeding us more of that, especially from advertisers. Facebook knows the kind of content you like better than you know yourself. And, as I mentioned earlier, Facebook has routinely made decisions and mistakes that just happen to serve its primary customers, advertisers, and not its users. I'll give a couple of brief examples.

Examples of Facebook Malpractice

In 2014, a study was conducted and published in the *Proceedings of the National Academy of Sciences* in which behavioral scientists worked with Facebook to intentionally manipulate the moods of people by delivering them overwhelming amounts of happy or sad content.[4] Robinson Meyer of *The Atlantic* reported: "For one week in January 2012, data scientists skewed what almost 700,000 Facebook users saw when they logged into its service. Some people were shown content with a preponderance of happy and positive words; some were shown content analyzed as sadder than average. And when the week was over, these manipulated users were more likely to post either especially positive or negative words themselves."[5]

Plenty of studies have been done throughout Facebook's history to examine the effects of Facebook use on human mental health and other aspects of our lives, but this was the first study that manipulated Facebook users and the content they saw to see what would happen. Facebook users were effectively virtual lab rats for a study on how social media affects mental health.

Many claimed that Facebook users were experimented on without their consent, but the grim reality is that the Facebook User Agreement we've all clicked to "accept" gives such consent. Likewise, Facebook is running experiments on the platform every single day. Mark Zuckerberg has said that ten thousand versions of Facebook are running every day.[6] When we click "accept" to Terms & Conditions or User Agreements, we are consenting to more than many of us realize. We may even be opening ourselves up to being manipulated by a foreign company or government.

As of the publication of this book, the most well-known Facebook privacy breach involves Cambridge Analytica and the 2016 United States presidential election.[7] In 2018 it was revealed that political consulting firm Cambridge Analytica harvested the data of millions of Facebook users through apps used on the platform and weaponized the data to manipulate people during a number of elections, including the 2016 United States presidential election.

The primary way they collected data was by creating a personality quiz app within Facebook through which they harvested the data of both the people who took the quiz and their friends. Cambridge Analytica used this data to influence a number of elections around the world, as beta tests, before they brought their operation to the United States. They primarily targeted people "more prone to impulsive anger or conspiratorial thinking than average citizens." Both Senator Ted Cruz and President Donald Trump paid $5 million to hire the firm to support their campaigns.[8]

Cambridge Analytica executives were also caught on hidden camera bragging about their ability to extort politicians by sending women to entrap them in sexual immorality. The Cambridge Analytica scandal demonstrates some of the most grievous real-world impacts loose privacy guidelines can have. Whether or not you're happy Donald Trump won the 2016 election, we ought to agree that what Cambridge Analytica did to manipulate Americans in the months preceding the election should not be allowed to happen again.

How to Protect Your Privacy

Before the birth of our daughter, my wife, Susie, and I decided that we would not post any pictures of her on the internet for an indefinite period of time after she was born. This decision upset some friends and family members who don't live nearby and can't see our daughter very often. A lot of people didn't understand why we were doing this. People tell us we are "weird" for not posting our daughter's picture online. They're right!

But think about that for a second. My wife and I are the weird ones because we don't post pictures of our toddler on the internet. If you told new parents in 2002, "In fewer than ten years it will be totally normal to post a picture of your toddler in the bathtub on the internet for the world to see," they would have looked at you like you were a huge creep. Today you're weird if you *don't* do that. It's crazy how quickly our expectations and norms change.

Susie and I have plenty of reasons we decided not to post pictures of our daughter online, and I don't need to go through all of those with you here. But the reason I share that is this: *to take privacy seriously today requires intentionality and may cause you to be "weird," if you can handle that.* Let me provide you with just a few practical ways you can be intentional about protecting your privacy online without having to stop using the internet completely.

Turn Location Services Off

Most social media apps will ask you to turn on Location Services to access special features associated with their platforms. Instagram, for instance, will let you add locations or local temperatures to your Stories if you have Location Services activated. Most people, wanting these location-based features, turn on location services without thinking twice. If you want to keep these apps from always knowing where you are, you should turn Location Services off and learn to live without those extra features.

Limit the Personal Information You Share

I have read a handful of stories over the years about people who had their homes robbed while on vacation because they boasted on Facebook about their ten-day Hawaiian excursion and someone with whom they were "friends" decided to take advantage of that information. Take some time and browse your social media profiles pretending you're a stranger coming across your page: What kind of information are you freely giving up about yourself? Is your address in the background of a Facebook profile picture? Did you accidentally take a picture of your credit card on the table when snapping a picture of your date night for Instagram? Could someone create a family tree of your entire living family based on profile information? Why would you willingly give this up? What do you gain? Pay attention to what you share about yourself.

Dig into Platform Privacy Settings

Most social media platforms you use have the ability to give you more privacy than you have by default. Platforms like Facebook do not make privacy settings strict by default because the more strictly you lock down your information, the less information can be gathered about you, and the less valuable advertisements are. Facebook, as an example, would be in a bad place financially if everyone on the platform turned on the most restrictive privacy settings they make available. But you can find settings that restrict the information Facebook gathers about you! Just navigate to the "Privacy" settings within Facebook and go through the different options.[9] You should do this on every app you have, frankly, whether or not it's social media.

I could list a dozen more ways to take control of your privacy on social media, but you can find those yourself if you want. One of the most common concerns I hear about the internet and privacy today is: "The government could track us and know everything about us." While we haven't seen an abuse of social media like that yet, is Facebook or Google tracking you and knowing everything about you that much better? What if we're so concerned about one privacy boogeyman that we've willingly embraced another?

These platforms have some features to support user privacy, but they only go so far. The only real way to free ourselves of the privacy violations we may experience via the social internet would be to abstain from the platforms completely. Most of us feel either unwilling or unable to do that. It's understandable. I would love to disconnect from the social internet completely when I think about the potential privacy violations, but I love too much of it to disconnect completely.

What is most important is that we recognize the poison in the water. We must be vigilant to recognize which platforms are more grievous offenders of our privacy than others. We must be willing to recognize that every click, tap, like, and comment is a drip, drip, drip of data we deposit into the vast well of data that many want to use for their profit and our loss.

The Cost We All Pay

Facebook is free. So are Instagram, Google, Twitter, and all of the other most common apps you use every day. But they come with great cost.

Using these platforms costs more than money. It costs us our privacy.

The revolution of the social internet is a bell we cannot unring. We cannot escape the social internet. It will be with us until the end of time. It is now the water in which we swim, and like fish, we simply can't exist outside of it. We can delete our accounts. We can revert to "dumb phones." But the social internet will persist, and it will infiltrate our lives in some way.

So, why have I spent an entire chapter explaining the privacy perils of an environment we can't escape? Because I want everyone reading this book to recognize that the social internet is not a neutral tool. The water in which we are swimming is poisoned. The sooner we recognize that, the sooner we will be able to resist manipulation from the platforms themselves or the people who abuse them.

The social internet doesn't cost us any money, but it might cost us our freedom and our minds. Further, from a Christian perspective, it's not like the Bible speaks specifically to "privacy as a human right." But I do think we should be conscious of how gross invasions of privacy can infringe upon the dignity we have as people made in the image of God. When people are viewed as little more than wells of data to be tapped for marketable information, it is hard to see them as beautiful beings made to reflect their Creator. The invasions of privacy we experience through the social internet are demeaning to our personhood. Let's be aware of this and, even if we don't disconnect completely, be more wary of what we share.

CHAPTER 6

We Pursue Affirmation Instead of Truth

Who killed JFK? Are they keeping aliens at Area 51? Did we actually go to the moon? Are powerful Americans trafficking children through a furniture company and a pizza parlor in Washington, D.C.? Was the coronavirus a plot to implant us all with microchips via a vaccine?

Conspiracy theories have been around for decades, and it should be noted that not all conspiracy theories are created equal. The most famous conspiracy theories in American history surround the possibility of extraterrestrial life at Area 51 and the assassination of President John F. Kennedy. These "conspiracy theories" are a bit less harmful to discuss than, say, the idea that Bill Gates created COVID-19 to implant Americans with a microchip via a vaccine. Discussing "who really killed JFK" is a little more innocuous than discussing whether to protect yourselves and others from a raging disease.

Though these conspiracy theories are different—and cause different degrees of harm—our fascination with all conspiracy theories is rooted in the same need: an explanation for the seemingly inexplicable. We see an inconsistency between the supposed simple cause of something and its massive, complex result.

Take the JFK assassination. It is hard to believe a single, lone gunman could cause as much havoc as was captured on the Zapruder film and in the time following the death of JFK. Surely there had to be some greater cause or force behind the killing of JFK than just a rogue guy with a gun . . . right? The fallout of the tragedy seems to outmatch its modest cause, which opens the door for a wide variety of greater, more conspiratorial reasons such a small act could have caused such a massive wave of change and sadness.

The ingredients of popular conspiracy theories vary based on the kinds of people who would be interested in them. Some people are more prone to believe conspiracy theories about sneaky government activity. Others are predisposed to conspiracy theories rooted in public health and the medical system. Yet others' ears are tickled by conspiracy theories surrounding religious groups and their secret maneuvers to seize power from world governments.

Part of the reason conspiracy theories have been so popular the last few decades is because, well, there has been a lot of *actual conspiracy*. If a *conspiracy* is defined as "a secret plan by a group or individual to do something unlawful or harmful," we are living in a time of conspiracy, aren't we? "Secret plans by groups or individuals to do something unlawful or harmful" would qualify Al Qaeda's attacks on 9/11 as a conspiracy, the Sandy Hook shooting by Adam Lanza as a conspiracy, and plenty of other acts of evil as conspiracy. Given the significant number of secret plans by groups of individuals to do something unlawful or harmful in the last two decades, it makes sense that many people are trying to conjure up theories of other, nonexistent conspiracies in an effort to explain the seemingly inexplicable. To summarize: a conspiracy is a secret plan to do evil, and a conspiracy theory is an allegation of a secret plan to do evil. With so many secret plans to do evil these days, the abundance of allegations of such activity, however outlandish or inaccurate, makes sense.

Why are we tempted to pass along conspiracy theories? We all recognize the brokenness of the world, and we have trouble believing that all of the death, destruction, and turmoil that surrounds us is simply the result of our collective sinful behavior. We recognize the tragic effects of sin on the world around us, and we think, *This has to be the coordinated effort of (fill in your favorite villain).* At the heart of conspiratorial thought is a desire to adequately address the problem of evil. We want to be able to explain why the world is as broken as it is, and it seems impossible that it could simply be because people are inherently bent toward violence, anger, and destruction.

How does social media act as a propellant for conspiracy theories? What is the social internet's role in the prevalence and fast spread of conspiracy theories today? Its role is central, not because the creators of the social media platforms we use want to support conspiracy theories, but because the base mechanisms of their platforms inherently connect people who think alike, want to consume content quickly, and cannot escape the anxiety that our broken world has etched on their hearts and minds.

> At the heart of conspiratorial thought is a desire to adequately address the problem of evil.

Social Media Propels Conspiracy Theories

Our desire to pursue comfort at the cost of truth is not new, but social media has made it much easier to hold tightly to a false narrative than it was to do so previously. Conspiracy theories existed long before the prevalence of the social internet, but it is foolish to deny that social media adds gasoline to the kindling fire of conspiracy theories. Max Read writes for *New York* magazine, "The intimate stage of social media, where vloggers and citizen journalists peddle theories without the baggage of these corrupted institutions, can appear to its users particularly direct, honest, and unmediated."[1] A simple understanding of the algorithms and other systems that make the social internet work leads to the undeniable conclusion that these platforms support the wildfire-like spread of conspiracy theories. Undergirding any "successful" conspiracy theory that gains traction online are two primary ingredients: (1) a lot of falsehoods (or "fake news") built on (2) an acorn of truth. Like every good lie, every good conspiracy theory is built on a small truth.

Social media has created an environment in which the falsehoods upon which a conspiracy theory is built spread a lot quicker than the small bit of truth on which it is built. Let's explore the two basic elements of the social internet environment that make it so easy for conspiracy theories (and other types of fake news) to spread.

> Like every good lie, every good conspiracy theory is built on a small truth.

Like-Minded Connection

The natural proclivity of almost everyone is to use social media to connect with others who think like we do. It would be great if it were natural for us to gravitate toward people with whom we disagree as quickly as we do to those with whom we agree, but we just don't. We primarily use social media to connect with people who have the same political, religious, and broadly ideological beliefs that we do.

It is normal that someone like me, an American Christian, would more frequently use social media to connect with other American Christians than with a French Muslim or an Indian Hindu. This isn't necessarily bad; it's just how humans are. We are tribal. Where this gets us into trouble, though, is when it creates a sort of tunnel-vision effect in which we are unable to see the world through the eyes of people who think, live, and believe differently than we do. This makes us prone to believe whatever our like-minded friends and family share on social media, without testing it against a reliable source of facts and information.

Social media is not designed for empathy, as I explained before. We only know what the world looks like from our virtual perch, and when we connect with a bunch of people who believe the same way we do, we are likely to have trouble discerning what is fact and what is our tribe's interpretation of fact, which may end up being more fictional than factual. This, naturally, makes us more likely to believe a conspiracy theory, however outlandish it may sound. We trust people who look, think, and live like us, and the internet has connected us to those kinds of people.

Quick, Engaging Content

When we're scrolling on our preferred social media platform, we like to consume a lot of content in a short period of time. We like short videos. We like clever memes. We like reading headlines. Most of us, when we're scrolling social media, don't stop to click a link and read an article before we like it or comment on it. This is a pet peeve of many social media managers who receive hateful comments from people who don't like the headline of an article and respond negatively without reading it (especially when doing so would probably reveal much that they like and agree with!).[2] These methods of content consumption set us up to be duped by deceiving headlines or outright false information.

Let's dive deeper into this by looking at Facebook because: (1) it's the most popular social media platform in the world, and (2) it's where conspiracy theories tend to spread most frequently online. Remember, Facebook's number-one goal is to make money, and they do that by collecting as much of our attention as they can and delivering ads in our news feeds.

In the business of monetizing our attention, Facebook does not have a preference toward serving us content that makes us happy or makes us mad. It just wants to make us feel *something*. Facebook doesn't care if you share a funny video that made you laugh or spend ten minutes typing an angry comment on a post you hated. It's all the same to Facebook because it kept your attention. The worst kind of content, in Facebook's eyes, is boring content. Content that makes you feel and act, whether in happiness or anger, is good; content that leaves you bored and scrolling, or leaving the site entirely, is bad.

Enter: conspiratorial content.

Conspiracy theory content is inherently polarizing and provocative. It's a sure bet to make you feel something. Facebook users are likely to engage with conspiracy theory content because they either find it reprehensible or agree with it.

The environment created by social internet platforms is a perfect environment for conspiracy theories to spread, even if the platforms would prefer they not spread at all. You simply cannot create a platform that monetizes data and attention *and* prevent the spread of attention-getting, emotion-inducing content. It's like hosting a birthday party with a bunch of teenage boys, laden with Mountain Dew and junk food. You may not host the party with the intent of replacing breakable objects in your house, but you're still probably going to have to do that. The creators of the social internet didn't set out to create an environment ripe for conspiracy theories to spread, but they have nonetheless.

Connecting the dots between "how social media works" and "why conspiracy theories spread" is not difficult. Conspiracy theories generate attention and engagement. Because conspiracy theories generate attention and engagement, they show up on a lot of feeds, and the result is a snowballing effect.

Let's examine a case study—a perfect example of how social media greases the tracks for powerful conspiracy theories to take hold in ways they never have before.

QAnon and Modern Social Media Conspiracy Theories

Edgar Welch didn't hurt anyone when he fired his AR-15 assault rifle into Comet Ping Pong, and the police arrested him without a fight. But why did Welch, a twenty-eight-year-old husband and father of two, drive six hours from his home in North Carolina to a pizzeria in Washington, D.C., on a Sunday in December 2016?

The internet told him that former Democratic presidential candidate Hillary Clinton and her campaign oversaw a child sex trafficking ring that operated, in part, out of Comet Ping Pong, the Washington, D.C., pizzeria. Specifically, Comet Ping Pong was alleged to be home to satanic ritual abuse of children. Welch, rightly wanting to protect children but wrongly believing what he read on the internet, took it upon himself to investigate. In the end, Welch found no evidence of the child abuse and trafficking about which he read online, and it was actually *he* who ended up facing justice—not the fictional child traffickers he set out to hunt.

This is "Pizzagate," as you may have heard it called, and it is one of the most consequential (and elaborate) conspiracy theories that has spread quickly across the country on the superhighway of social media.[3] Really, the Pizzagate conspiracy theory is just one small part of QAnon, a far-right conservative political movement built upon the idea that a group of celebrities and Democrat politicians were leading a deep-state effort to undermine former president Donald Trump and are trafficking children for the purpose of sexual or satanic ritual abuse.

QAnon is most simply understood as a political movement, but it is probably most accurately understood as a political cult, as its adherents demonstrate markedly religious tendencies. QAnon and the numerous tentacles of conspiracy theories that orbit around the movement collectively demonstrate the seismic effect of social media on the spread and legitimization of conspiracy theories.

The QAnon movement is built around an anonymous person who has identified himself as "Q" across a number of the deepest, darkest corners of the social internet (4chan, 8chan, 8kun, and others). Adrienne LaFrance summarizes the general beliefs of those who adhere to QAnon like this:

> Q is an intelligence or military insider with proof that corrupt world leaders are secretly torturing children all over the world; the malefactors are embedded in the deep state; Donald Trump is working tirelessly to thwart them. ("These people need to ALL be ELIMINATED," Q wrote in one post.) The eventual destruction of the global cabal is imminent, Q prophesies, but can be accomplished only with the support of patriots who search for meaning in Q's clues. To believe Q requires rejecting mainstream institutions, ignoring government officials, battling apostates, and despising the press. One of Q's favorite rallying cries is "You are the news now." Another is "Enjoy the show," a phrase that his disciples regard as a reference to a coming apocalypse: When the world as we know it comes to an end, everyone's a spectator.[4]

The message of Q aligns nicely with the anti-media, anti-establishment, and anti-liberal platform of the far-right end of the American political spectrum. But how do the conspiratorial ramblings of an anonymous social-media user make it from the darkest corners of the social internet to your grandma's Facebook feed or even to the White House? How does an anonymous post about child sex trafficking on a sketchy message board eventually lead a man to arm himself, drive six hours, and investigate?

Because we seek affirmation on the internet at the cost of the truth.

QAnon is powerful because Q makes many predictive statements that, like a horoscope, are so vague they can be interpreted as accurate by anyone who wishes to believe they are the oracles of a prophet. Q creates social media content in corners of the social internet in which there are more conspiracy theorists than there are people with common sense. It's like dropping a match in the driest part of a forest—nothing will keep the fire from igniting. Then the theories spread from the dark corners of the internet in which they originate to more popular social media platforms, like Facebook and Twitter, where they are injected into groups and feeds of people who are predisposed to believe them because of their political beliefs.

Because social media platforms are designed to connect like-minded people, injecting the prophecies of Q into the social media feeds of the right people is easy. The theories then spread on the most used internet websites in the world, eventually making their way into dinner table conversation, White House press briefings, and perhaps leading people to take matters into their own hands—like Edgar Welch did in 2016 or like hundreds of Americans did on January 6, 2021.

The Pizzagate incident in 2016 made the wider world more aware of the real-world effects of an internet-based political cult like QAnon, and it was but a taste of the tumult that QAnon would unleash by its organization of the siege on the United States Capitol on January 6, 2021. Political and national security concerns of the Capitol attack aside, the events of that day opened the eyes of many people to the reality that the bizarre-sounding threats of violence one may come across on the internet are to be taken seriously. People who had been studying the messaging of QAnon and other related extremists on the internet for years, like journalists Ben Collins and Brandy Zadrozny of NBC News, were not caught off-guard by what happened on January 6, however shocking it may have been. The two reporters wrote on January 8, just two days after the insurrection:

> On the fringe message board 8kun, which is popular with QAnon followers, for example, users talked for weeks about a siege of the Capitol, some talking about it like a fore-gone conclusion. Others simply debated how violent the uprising should be, and if police should be exempt.
>
> "You can go to Washington on Jan 6 and help storm the Capital," said one 8kun user a day before the siege. "As many Patriots as can be. We will storm the government buildings, kill cops, kill security guards, kill

federal employees and agents, and demand a recount."[5]

The conspiracy to attempt to siege the Capitol was also discussed in the wide open on more prominent, mainstream social media platforms like Facebook. The profound spread of conspiracy theories and the underlying, common desire to be comforted and affirmed at the cost of truth are easily perpetuated by algorithms and features that promote engagement with no regard for reality.

QAnon has capitalized on the tribalism and resultant tunnel vision the modern social internet fosters by whipping people into a frenzy with falsehoods that, though false, support the beliefs of a particular group of passionate people who use social media with zeal. People love to consume and share content that supports their belief systems, regardless of whether that content has any basis in fact.

> People love to consume and share content that supports their belief systems, regardless of whether that content has any basis in fact.

A Call to Critical Thinking

Wanting to pursue comfort or affirmation at the cost of truth has never been easier. Social media has created an environment in which everyone is a reporter and the news can be whatever you want it to be. In the middle of the twentieth century, the majority of Americans received their news from the same person: Walter Cronkite. Today, virtually half of Americans receive their news from their Facebook or Twitter feeds, which are often meticulously curated to align reality with their beliefs.

Social media echo chambers are real. Even if these echo chambers aren't always the primary cause of polarization, they can still warp our understanding of what is real. When we use social media primarily to connect with people who agree with our worldview, we only consume content that adheres to our worldview, leading us to distrust those who do not share our worldview. This often leads us to trust those who share our worldview without considering the veracity of their claims. This is how our addiction to the social internet has crippled our critical thinking and led us to assume that reality is whatever our curated feeds tell us it is.

As users of the social internet, we must be aware we have, whether intentionally or unintentionally, curated our content feeds with content that supports, or at least does not contradict, the way we see the world. With that understanding, we should evaluate every piece of content we see with a critical eye.

Because most of us are lazy content consumers, we often see memes making fun of a politician we don't like or head-lines that confirm our beliefs and assume they are based in fact. We ought not make such an assumption. Let's stop being lazy content consumers on social media and start caring about whether what we are reading is true.

For my Christian readers, who else should be more interested in pursuing the truth than us? To lazily scroll through our feeds and gluttonously gobble up comfortable content is the height of foolishness and far from the biblical standard of wisdom and Christlikeness to which we have been called.

I fear that we are so interested in being affirmed and ideologically coddled that, even though we recognize much of the content on our feeds is false, we simply don't care because this content supports our understanding of how the world *should be*. When it comes down to it, our insidious desire to create virtual pseudo realities is a modern manifestation of one of our earliest sins: the idolatrous pursuit of making gods of ourselves, abandoning the truth for a shadow of it.

In its early days, the social internet felt like a sort of parallel, subservient reality to our off-line lives. Who we were online was a muted, semi-accurate, not-quite-full picture of who we were off-line. Our lives off-line were primary, and what we chose to communicate online flowed downstream from our fuller lives off-line. I fear, however, that this is no longer the case.

My fear is that our online lives have become lenses through which we view our off-line lives, and our off-line lives are no longer primary but secondary. As Bo Burnham says in *Inside*: "The non-digital world is merely a theatrical space in which one stages and records content for the much more real, much more vital digital space."[6]

In 2008, if you came across a story on the internet about politicians trafficking children, you would have been skeptical and checked with off-line sources. Today, if you come across a story on the internet about politicians trafficking children, from sources you've grown to trust (because they confirm your prior assumptions), it is more likely to define your reality—a reality no off-line fact-checkers can convince you to change. We have become so addicted to the social internet and the steady diet of content that aligns to our beliefs that we eat up whatever we're fed without checking if it's laced with poison.

Worse, we have come to like the taste of the poison, and no one can take away our freedom to consume it.

CHAPTER 7

We Demonize People We Dislike

I n many corners of the social internet, a lie lingers that "people who disagree with me cause me harm." Believing this lie leads us to demonize people we dislike. The most common fruit of believing this lie could be characterized as *cancel culture*, a term popularized in the last decade whose meaning is often in the eye of the beholder. We will explore more about cancel culture in the next chapter, but right now we need to examine the building blocks of intolerance that cause us to try to expel people from the internet.

I am not a political scientist, but in order to understand conflict on the social internet today, it's important to recognize the political contexts that drive so much of the conflict we either experience or observe online. An important distinction should be made between what we will call "traditional liberalism" and "progressive liberalism." Traditional liberalism in America allows for a wide variety of perspectives and ideologies to flourish. Progressive liberalism that is more extreme in its social aspects and tends to flourish on the social internet today is less welcoming to a plethora of perspectives and ideologies. Where traditional liberalism was dogmatic in its promotion of an open marketplace of many ideas, modern, progressive liberalism is often dogmatic in its promotion of progressive ideologies only, with no interest in creating an open marketplace of ideas for progressive and conservative ideologies to live together.

Part of the reason the intolerant progressive liberalism flourishes on the social internet is the same reason extremist conservatism flourishes on the social internet—it is easier to rile up extremists on either side of the political spectrum than it is to rile up moderates. Moderates, by nature of their even-handed approach and openness to various perspectives, are not as loud on the social internet and, therefore, don't build up as much of a following as more passionate users who take more extreme views. The social internet, in terms of political and social ideologies, is best used to whip into a frenzy those who are already most zealous, and the most zealous often hold the most polarizing, extreme views.

The lie that "people who disagree with me cause me harm" is a form of safetyism that is an effort to protect against a false, or overstated, feeling of fragility. In their book *The Coddling of the American Mind*, which will be cited throughout this chapter, Jonathan Haidt and Greg Lukianoff explore all of the different factors that have contributed to the lie that "people who disagree with me cause me harm." Three of the major factors that prop up this false belief are: (1) a culture of safety-ism, (2) an overestimation of our fragility, and (3) our inability to give others the benefit of the doubt. Haidt and Lukianoff break down these factors in a number of contexts, most often in higher education contexts, and I think it would be helpful for us to see how these factors relate to the social internet and its reinforcement of the lie that "disagreement equals harm."

It's Okay to Feel Unsafe

At the heart of the social internet are words and the exchange of words between people. Whether those words are tweets, blog posts, YouTube videos, or other forms of content, the heart of the social internet is the exchange of words across a wide variety of audio, visual, and text mediums.

It is important that we consider carefully how we use our words. We ought to be intentional about using our words to build others up rather than tear them down. Throughout the book of Proverbs, we see the power of our words and the responsibility we have to wield them with wisdom and care. Here are just a few such pieces of Scripture:

> "With his mouth the ungodly destroys his neighbor, but through knowledge the righ-teous are rescued." (Prov. 11:9)

"A gentle answer turns away anger, but a harsh
word stirs up wrath." (Prov. 15:1)

"Death and life are in the power of the tongue,
and those who love it will eat its fruit." (Prov.
18:21)

We should also be intentional about using our words to
advocate for what we believe is right, even if others may interpret this advocacy as an attack on their way of thinking or
living. How we use our words on the social internet matters,
and we ought to avoid causing unnecessary offense as much as
we can in how we conduct ourselves online.

However, a significant disagreement exists about where the
line falls between *necessary* and *unnecessary* offensive speech.
This has long been the case—it is not a new issue—but the
sheer volume of speech being exchanged on the social internet today has made vehement disagreements about "harmful
speech" a daily debate for some.

In *The Coddling of the American Mind*, Haidt (author,
sociologist at New York University) and Lukianoff (president and attorney at Foundation for Individual Rights in
Education) spend a significant amount of ink examining how
safetyism, cancel culture, and other modern liberal practices
have changed college campuses, and what parental and cultural factors may have led to such actions.

Lukianoff has spent his career defending free speech on
college campuses. He began this career in 2001. Back then
professors were often the censors and students the free speech

adherents. By the 2010s, Lukianoff noticed a shift occurring: professors now advocated for free speech, and students were advocating for more censorship. A bevy of societal shifts altered the foundation of American campus life—and of the culture of young people in general—between the early 2000s and the 2010s, but one of the most prominent was the pervasiveness of the social internet and the interconnectedness it provided.

"Safetyism," as explained by Haidt and Lukianoff, "refers to a culture or belief system in which safety has become a sacred value, which means that people become unwilling to make trade-offs demanded by other practical and moral concerns. 'Safety' trumps everything else, no matter how unlikely or trivial the potential danger."[1]

Because Haidt and Lukianoff primarily work in higher education, most of their examples of how safetyism is expressed in culture are cited from those experiences. The authors come to the conclusion that, for a variety of reasons, many of today's college students and recent college graduates have been imbued with the idea that ideologies and worldviews that are incompatible with their own are potentially "harmful" and must be silenced. Haidt and Lukianoff ask the question: "Should college students interpret emotional pain as a sign that they are in danger?"[2] Likewise, should social media users interpret disagreement or even vulgar, rude comments as "dangerous"? Jean Twenge writes in her book *iGen*, which analyzes a variety of cultural phenomena surrounding those born since 1995, that these young people have been taught,

"One should be safe not just from car accidents and sexual assault but from people who disagree with you."[3] Protecting ourselves from unnecessary physical, mental, or other kinds of violence and harm are important, but disparities in ideologies and worldview ought not be categorized as "potentially damaging or harmful."

The connection between this phenomenon and the social internet is clear. If a generation of young people—the people who spend the most time engaging on the social internet—has been raised to believe that people who disagree with them are potentially harming them, they will grow to believe it is their moral responsibility to silence any disagreement and remove dissenters from public discourse. This has led to the proliferation of cancel culture, which we briefly defined before and will explore in more depth shortly. For now we need to study a companion problem that persists alongside safetyism: an overestimation of our fragility.

We Are Not as Fragile as We Think

Musician Rich Mullins was right when he wrote his song "We Are Not As Strong As We Think We Are." But we are not as fragile as we think we are, either. We are all weak in some ways, whether because of genetics, personal experiences, or otherwise. The world is broken, evil and violence run amok, and we ought to be aware of what can hurt us and how to protect ourselves and our loved ones against undue harm. However, as we keep watch for anyone or anything that may harm us or those we love, we must realize we are not fragile. Rather, we are *antifragile*.

In his book *Antifragile*, Nassim Nicholas Taleb sorts everything there is into three categories: fragile, resilient, and antifragile.[4] A glass vase is fragile because it is easily broken and cannot fix itself. My solid wood desk is resilient because it can withstand significant pressure without breaking, but the pressure doesn't make the table any stronger. Human muscles are antifragile because they need adversity and pressure in order to become stronger and grow; without being stretched, human muscles become weak.

Humans, like the muscles in their bodies, are antifragile. We need adversity throughout our lives to make us stronger. Obviously, some kinds of adversity do not leave us stronger but rather leave us broken and in a worse state than we were before. We ought not have to endure a horrific car accident or rampant emotional abuse from a parent in order to grow into the strong people we were meant to be. But we do need to endure some measure of disagreements, conflicts, and social strife so that we might learn, adapt, and grow.

> Humans, like the muscles in their bodies, are antifragile. We need adversity throughout our lives to make us stronger.

In this way our innumerable interactions with people on the social internet who believe differently than we do could be seen as a tremendous gift! Social media is rife with conflict and disagreement—which could actually help us learn how to defend and articulate what we believe in more concise, coherent ways. In this way the social internet can act like an ever-present crucible, refining the pillars of our worldviews.

Unfortunately, many have instead decided that social media is not a refining fire in which we might hone our beliefs. Rather, they have decided that the disagreement and conflict present on the social internet are actually acts of violence that put people, especially marginalized people, in harm's way. That is not to say social media has not led to legitimate, long-lasting harm for people—it certainly has. But this harm has not come at the hands of the good-faith presentation of a sincerely held worldview; rather it has come from incessant bullying or threats that are genuinely meant to terrorize other users. While we should never ignore the reality of online harassment that can easily lead to tragic consequences, we should be careful not to call any expression of disagreement "harmful."

We have adopted an ethic of safetyism because we overestimate how mentally, physically, and emotionally fragile we are. Because we think we are fragile, we adopt a culture that makes safety a top priority. What happens, then, is we create a self-fulfilling prophecy. Overprotection for fear of being fragile actually makes us *more* fragile because we lack exposure to small, daily adversities that may make us stronger and more prepared to endure a more life-changing adversity that may come later in life.

The problem Haidt and Lukianoff have identified in their experiences on college campuses is as present on the social internet as it is a college campus because the same people dominate both environments. A generation of young people who were either being born or learning basic arithmetic around September 11, 2001, were taught by their parents and teachers that safety is of the utmost importance. This cultural inculcation mixed with the modern liberalism of ideological intolerance that runs rampant among young people today has created an environment in which "disagreeing with me violates the value I hold most dear: my safety."

So, how might we practically push back against the lie that disagreement is harmful? By giving people with whom we disagree the benefit of the doubt, even if they haven't earned it. In a social media conflict, someone has to take the first step toward kindness and peace. Why shouldn't that be you and me?

Give Others the Benefit of the Doubt

In my professional life I spent years advising a large Christian publishing organization on social media strategy and helping execute that strategy. In that time one of my most consistent pieces of advice was this: "Before you post anything on social media, read it through the lens of someone who *wants* to misinterpret you. Ask yourself: 'What's the worst possible way this can be interpreted?' and make appropriate edits to guard against willful misinterpretation."

This advice may sound cynical or pessimistic, but I promise you that those who work in a role in which they have to represent a brand on social media in front of hundreds of thousands of people agree with me. Why? Because anyone who has spent a significant amount of time overseeing social media for a major brand knows that many on social media make it their mission to willfully misinterpret social media content posted by brands in an effort to undermine them.

But this reality isn't unique to brands' social media. People do this to other people all the time.

Most social media conflict isn't started by good-faith disagreement; it's started because someone chose to interpret the content of another user in a way that might ignite a conflict. Willful misinterpretation and refusing to give others on social media the benefit of the doubt is actually more consistent with the goal of most online conflict than is attempting to understand others, giving them the benefit of the doubt. For many, the purpose of social media conflict is to make a scene and perpetuate the conflict, not to resolve it. To dive into all of the possible psychological or sociological reasons people would rather perpetuate conflict on social media than solve it would be a bit outside the scope of this book (and the expertise of its author!). Rather, let's briefly explore why giving others the benefit of the doubt is an important step in pushing back against our tendency to demonize people we dislike or with whom we disagree.

The term *microaggression* was popularized in a 2007 article by Columbia University Teacher's College professor Derald

Wing Sue, who defines *microaggressions* as "brief and commonplace daily verbal, behavioral, or environmental indignities, whether intentional or unintentional, that communicate hostile, derogatory, or negative racial slights and insults toward people of color."[5] According to Google Trends, the topic of "microaggression" has increased in popularity over time and is at its peak all-time interest at the writing of this book.

Without a doubt, we should do all we can to not intentionally hurt or offend people who look, live, or believe differently than we do. Whether using explicit hate speech or making inaccurate assumptions based on stereotypes, we should do all we can to avoid bringing unnecessary offense to others. But here's the problem with Sue's definition of a microaggression: *aggression, by definition, is never unintentional or accidental!*

Our public discourse, especially on social media, has reached a point at which someone may be interpreted as aggressive when they simply make a mistake or are (often willfully) misinterpreted. It is not a good idea always to be interpreting others' actions as malicious, but this is what we do on social media all the time. And again, the reason we assume the worst about people and read their actions as uncharitably as possible is because, whether or not we admit it, we often *want* the social media conflict to continue, not find resolution.

What is important for us, as we try to understand the waters of the social internet in which we swim, is to recognize that others will likely willfully misinterpret what we say and assume the worst about us while we do all we can not to reciprocate. We ought to be wise to the destructive ways of the social internet while not perpetuating them—as wise as serpents and as innocent as doves, as Scripture says. When we find ourselves in a social media conflict created by willful misinterpretation, we ought to assume the best of the other and take the conflict off-line so that it can be resolved privately and not in front of an audience—which may tempt either party to perform for their supporters. For those of us who consider ourselves followers of Christ, the great Peacemaker, we ought to be the first to work to resolve any social media conflict because we assume the best of others.

However, let's be clear: to assume the best of others does not mean we should be naive to what their intentions may be. When we find ourselves in social media conflict, we ought to assume the best of others, that they don't mean ill, with the full understanding of the fact that we *could* be wrong, and they *could* mean ill. We approach social media conflict with the *understanding* that ill-intent is possible without the *assumption* that it is present.

Let's Be Better

"People who disagree with me cause me harm" is one of the more insidious lies swimming in the waters of the social internet, and it leads us to demonize those we dislike or those with whom we disagree. The lie is built on the idea that differences of belief, politics, or mere opinion can cause damage to other people. We ought not treat people as bigots when they do not appear to be acting in malice or with ill-intent, even if we find their views reprehensible. Indeed, hate speech and rudeness should not be accepted, but the idea that sincere disagreement causes harm or violence is unhealthy and inaccurate.

As we work to improve the social internet waters in which we swim, let's do what we can to give others the benefit of the doubt and not assume the worst of people with whom we disagree. Even people who believe very differently about the most foundational truths of life should be treated with respect and dignity. We ought not treat people with contempt or claim they are victimizing us simply because they have different worldviews than we do.

Unfortunately, our tendency to demonize people with whom we disagree has led to another damaging trend: we attempt to destroy the people we demonize by "canceling" them . . . or worse.

CHAPTER 8

We Destroy People We Demonize

When users of the social internet are swept up in the lie that "people who disagree with me cause me harm," it is only natural that another lie follows it in its wake: "We must dismantle the lives of harmful people." When we demonize people we dislike or with whom we disagree, it is natural (because of sin) that we then seek to destroy such people.

Our desire to destroy those whom we dislike is most commonly recognized as "cancel culture," which has only come to prominence in the last few years and has, unfortunately and like everything else, been politicized. But before we dive into picking apart the good, bad, and ugly of cancel culture, we ought to ask the question more broadly: "Why are people nasty on the social internet?"

Really, this goes back to the premise of chapter 4: attention is the currency of the internet, and nastiness gets the most attention. When we all get together online and the only currency is attention, we will stop at nothing to acquire as much of that currency as possible, and the best way to do that is to create conflict.

The general atmosphere of nastiness on the social internet is primarily generated by the reality that attention is the currency of the social internet, and nastiness is an easy get-rich-quick scheme because it's the simplest way to harvest the most attention. But believing the lie that "we must dismantle the lives of harmful people" follows closely in the wake of believing the lie that "people who disagree with me cause me harm" because of a connecting belief that "the only way to receive justice for the harm done to me is to cause harm in return."

> Attention is the currency of the internet, and nastiness gets the most attention.

A variety of factors have created an environment on the social internet in which the slightest offense or ideological disagreement can be interpreted as a form of "violence" or "harm." What follows, then, is a desire to find justice for the harm done. This theoretical pursuit of justice is often just a pursuit of vengeance in disguise. The offended will often stop at nothing to dismantle the life of the offender in the name of "justice" and "accountability." In the end the goal is to silence, humiliate, and "cancel" the offender as a form of justice for the offended. This series of events has been repeated so often that an entire culture has been formed around its existence. We will call it "cancel culture."[1]

What Is Cancel Culture?

The phrase *cancel culture* first started appearing on the internet in the early 2010s, but it didn't really start to gain traction until around 2017. One of the earliest manifestations of cancel culture before the term was even popularized was a Tumblr blog called "Your Fave Is Problematic" and other similar blogs, which explored various celebrities and entertainers and how they held views or lived in ways that were "problematic," or morally suspect, usually from a more progressive ideological perspective. The act of "canceling" and the "cancel culture" phenomenon most commonly plays out in Twitter's corner of the social internet, so much of our discussion this chapter will focus there. However, it should be noted that in particularly serious cases of cancel culture, in which a high-profile figure has allegedly committed a heinous crime, the call to cancel the offender will spill over to other social platforms like Instagram and YouTube. (Few high-profile examples of cancel culture have played out on Facebook, from what I have researched and observed.) "Canceling" people on the internet has been happening since before "cancel culture" became a household term. So let's explore what it means to "cancel" someone more broadly, then we will zero in on cancel culture as a more modern phenomenon.

Being "canceled" on the internet can result in a wide variety of outcomes, often depending on how well-known the canceled person is, the nature of their alleged "crime," and how many people are campaigning for them to be canceled. An attempt to cancel someone could be as silly as friends publicly calling out another friend on social media because of a gross habit, like dipping steak in ketchup. Such a cancelation may look like this: "At dinner tonight, Steve literally dipped his $30 steak in ketchup. Steve can't have steak anymore. #CancelSteve."

Or, at the more serious end of the cancel spectrum, a celebrity could be accused of a serious transgression against the law or progressive ideals, like making jokes about race or sexuality. Actor and comedian Kevin Hart experienced this more serious brand of canceling in 2018 when he was announced as the host of the Oscars. Social media users recalled jokes Hart made in previous comedy performances that they categorized as "homophobic" and called for him not to be the host of the awards show and to apologize. Hart eventually apologized and refused to host the show, despite being asked to still host it. We'll explore more of Hart's experience later.

To summarize: canceling someone can be a goofy way to call out a friend for some lighthearted *faux pas*, or it can be a way to "hold accountable" some of the most famous people in the world for their transgression of the progressive cultural orthodoxy. What has followed from repeated canceling on social media is a culture in which canceling is often a recognized form of justice.

In a 2019 piece for *Vox* titled "Why We Can't Stop Fighting about Cancel Culture," writer Aja Romano defines "cancel culture" like this: "A celebrity or other public figure does or says something offensive. A public backlash, often fueled by politically progressive social media, ensues. Then come the calls to cancel the person—that is, to effectively end their career or revoke their cultural cachet, whether through boycotts of their work or disciplinary action from an employer."[2]

Romano's definition is a better definition of *canceling* more broadly, but the repeated execution of what Romano describes is what has created cancel culture.

It has become broadly acceptable for social media users to engage in canceling celebrities who are "problematic" because it has been recognized by media outlets and in public perception as a form of "accountability" or "justice." Because Twitter tends to be more dominated by progressive voices, especially media figures, holding views or taking actions that do not align with more progressive ideals is what often gets celebrities, or even common citizens, canceled.

Over time, as cancel culture has gained more of a foothold in broader culture, dismantling someone's life because of something they have said or done has extended far beyond the most rich, famous, powerful people. Today even normal people who are caught on camera acting in an objectionable way may be canceled if enough noise is made. Someone who berates a grocery store clerk or calls the cops unnecessarily may be tried before the social media jury for being "problematic," which can lead to their being harassed on- and off-line, often being fired from their jobs.

In cancel culture, what was once viewed as "holding the powerful accountable" has now morphed into something much more nefarious. It often looks as much like mob justice as anything.

But before we explore the negative consequences of cancel culture in more depth, we need to examine the ways in which cancel culture has provided some benefit. The negative far outweighs the positive, to be sure, but there is at least one positive effect of cancel culture we shouldn't ignore.

The Positive Effect of Cancel Culture

When I think about the positive effect of cancel culture, the old adage comes to mind: "A broken clock is right twice a day." Generally speaking, cancel culture is cancerous. It is, in my view, a modern form of mob justice that caters to the cowardly and lazy who are willing to grab virtual torches and pitchforks but wouldn't be willing to grab actual torches and pitchforks if it came down to it.

As we talked about with tribalism a few chapters ago, it costs so little to grab virtual torches and pitchforks. The barrier to entry is so low to enter into the online outrage culture that naturally flows into cancel culture, we ought to view any attempt to dismantle the lives of people by way of a social media mob with a critical eye. Evil people should be held accountable, by all means, but pursuing mob justice on a rude Starbucks customer through a Twitter hashtag feels a bit . . . inappropriate.

However, given all of that, we need to acknowledge what cancel culture gets right: the powerful being held accountable by those who are not as powerful. The clearest manifestation of the powerful being held accountable by those who are not powerful via a cancel culture movement on social media is the #MeToo movement.

While the #MeToo movement didn't actually start online—it was started as a nonprofit movement in 2016—it largely played out on social media in the years following its inception. The #MeToo movement, which was burning hottest in 2017–2018, but hasn't really "stopped" even to this day, provides a way for millions of sexual assault survivors around the world to share their stories in solidarity with one another against their more powerful sexual abusers.

Some may not classify the #MeToo movement as a manifestation of cancel culture, but it most certainly is. In fact, it is undoubtedly the crown jewel of cancel culture! How is it cancel culture? It is a major social media movement in which millions of social media users hold powerful people accountable for their actions, often resulting in their removal from their posts of cultural influence. Major Hollywood figures, politicians, religious figures, and others in positions of power are rightly called out, often on social media, for their sexual malpractice in the recent or distant past and rightly removed from their positions of power.

At the root of the #MeToo movement, and what makes it one of the only real positive examples of cancel culture, is that the #MeToo movement gives vulnerable people a way to band together and hold accountable the powerful people who abused them. This is valuable and indicative of an even broader populist phenomenon. In many ways, the social internet has given a voice to the common people. This is apparent on Facebook where conservative voices thrive, and it is apparent on Twitter where more progressive voices thrive. The social internet has provided a way for millions of people around the world to connect with others. From this connection will come a sharing of positive and negative experiences. When millions of people around the world connect and different groups of people recognize that they have been abused or otherwise poorly treated by a person in power, those people will band together in support of one another as they attempt to evict the powerful abuser from his or her position of influence. This is, I think, a good development.

Historically, a powerful Hollywood elite like Harvey Weinstein could get away with sexual abuse because he was powerful and his victims believed they were alone, as they feared sharing their experiences. But with the ability to connect with others via the social internet, they were able to recognize their solidarity.

It is easy for a powerful person to abuse an individual so long as the individual believes he or she is alone in his or her abusive experience. It is difficult for a powerful person to oppress the weak when the weak can band together and topple the powerful as a collective force.

Cancel culture has allowed the weak to hold the powerful accountable. That is most apparent in the #MeToo movement and the other related movements that have followed in its wake. The powerful should be held accountable, and the social internet provides an avenue for that accountability. Praise God!

Unfortunately, cancel culture isn't used for good-faith efforts to hold the powerful accountable for criminality or other broadly unacceptable conduct as often as it is used to indict people on "problematic" conduct as defined by those who hold to progressive ideals. This is another reason I point to the #MeToo movement as a positive effect of cancel culture: it is a response to *actual* harm. Sexual abuse is not the kind of ordinary, daily resistance that strengthens naturally antifragile human beings; it is a vile, repulsive, damaging violation of a human being made in God's image, and it should be addressed accordingly.

> It is difficult for a powerful person to oppress the weak when the weak can band together and topple the powerful as a collective force.

Yet not all of cancel culture is a response to a real injustice like the #MeToo movement. Instead, people begin to conflate "holding the powerful accountable for their oppression and abuse" and "dismantling the lives of people who hurt my feelings or disagree with me." What results is a sloppy form of mob justice that helps no one and serves to perpetuate outrage.

The Negative Consequences of Cancel Culture

Cancel culture bears the fruit of vengeance more than it bears the fruit of justice. Why? Because in order for justice to be achieved by rallying a mob of angry onlookers on the internet, the "cancelee," if you will, has to have actually committed an act of injustice that needs to be reconciled.

Sometimes this is the case, as we saw with the #MeToo movement, and the cancelees are brought to justice either in the public eye or in the criminal courts. But most of the time, canceling people doesn't result in justice at all; it just results in a modern, real-life rendition of the Two Minutes Hate George Orwell wrote into *1984*, in which people watch a video of a political foe and express their collective hatred for him. The Two Minutes Hate is described in *1984*: "A hideous ecstasy of fear and vindictiveness, a desire to kill, to torture, to smash faces in with a sledge hammer, seemed to flow through the whole group of people like an electric current, turning one even against one's will into a grimacing, screaming lunatic."[3] This sounds eerily like the atmosphere of cancel culture, including the threats of death for the recipient of the collective hate.

What makes cancel culture lead to more negative consequences than positive results of justice and redemption? Why does it feel like cancel culture creates a lot of noise on social media but rarely results in any demonstrable, constructive change off-line? Let's look at four primary factors: (1) subjective morality, (2) no incentive for reconciliation, (3) unclear objectives/demands, and (4) no realistic means of follow-up.

Subjective Morality

A major reason cancel culture often has a difficult time exacting lasting, effective change in the real world is because there isn't a shared morality on which a case for canceling someone may be built. It's easy to cancel people for actions they have taken that compromise basic human decency—relatively few people came to the defense of Harvey Weinstein or others accused of sexual misconduct. This is because most people consider the crimes Weinstein and others committed as clearly worthy of career cancellation, criminal justice, and cultural ostracism.

The stickiness comes with all of the other reasons people are canceled on the internet that aren't so cut-and-dried. Some adults are canceled for tweets they sent when they were in their teens. Others are being canceled for holding a biblical, or "traditional," sexual ethic. Others are canceled for offenses that may have been unintentional or ambiguous. When people are canceled for reasons less than criminal, the cancelation struggles to gain momentum and stick because not everyone agrees someone's life should be dismantled for views or actions that fall within the realm of "decent," even if they are unkind or otherwise objectionable.

No Incentive for Reconciliation

This is a big reason cancel culture results in a lot of noise but not a lot of change. In many corners of the social internet, conflict is incentivized. Why? Because, as we've seen, conflict often yields the most attention. Attempting to cancel someone is, without a doubt, a "conflict," and it draws a lot of attention. The fight is where the value lies. Those who attempt to cancel someone have no incentive in accepting an apology or reconciling the situation. Why? Because when the conflict is resolved, attention evaporates. Most times, the only acceptable result is the dismantling of the cancelee's life. No forgiveness is possible. No reconciliation accepted. To forgive or attempt to reconcile would undermine the true goal of cancellation: vengeance.

Unclear Objectives/Demands

One of the saddest parts of someone getting canceled is watching them attempt to appease the crowd of people armed with virtual torches and pitchforks. Kevin Hart told Stephen Colbert in an interview after he had been canceled by people on social media and opted out of hosting the Oscars: "No matter how many times you keep peeling it back, it's just endless. I apologized, 'Apologize again!' I said I apologized before, 'Apologize after that apology!' It just keeps going." Hart is lamenting the fact that every time he felt like he met the demands of the mob, they kept moving the goalposts.

This is a common function of a cancel culture mob. The mob creates a list of demands, often an apology and some act demonstrating a change of heart. Then, once the cancelee meets the list of demands, the mob is not satisfied and creates another list of demands that are more difficult, if not impossible, to meet. Why would they do this? Refer to point two—they have no incentive for reconciliation.

No Realistic Means of Follow-Up

The last major factor in why cancel culture creates more noise than change is a pretty simple one: an online mob who calls for change in the life of someone they do not know has no realistic means of following up with the person to determine if real change has occurred. If a mob of angry people online cancels a celebrity for an offensive tweet from a decade prior, and the celebrity apologizes and promises not to make similar offensive remarks again, how can the mob hold the person accountable? Sure, they can keep an eye on the celebrity's tweets, but the celebrity could just make the same offensive comments off-line, right? How would the mob know?

This is why, in my view, cancel culture mobs rarely stop short of dismantling the lives of the people they attempt to cancel. Because the mob has no reliable means of holding the people they cancel accountable

> Cancel culture mobs rarely stop short of dismantling the lives of the people they attempt to cancel.

for change, they assume change will not come, so they try to ruin the canceled as much as possible, just to be sure they have paid for what they have done.

Our Pursuit of Justice

Deep within us all is a desire for justice. We want people to be held accountable for their reprehensible actions so they don't hurt others and do their part in maintaining a civil, kind world. This is a good desire, and Christians would argue it is evidence of the image of God in us. Our God is a just God, and because we are made in His image, we want to see justice in our broken world. Unfortunately, the social internet has created an environment in which users attempt to take justice into their own hands, playing the role of a pretentious hall monitor on the internet, using their own set of rules to determine who has stepped out of line and who hasn't.

The bar for what is "harmful" on the internet is lower than it has ever been. The desire to pursue justice is as high as it has been in a generation. This deadly combination has created a culture in which it is acceptable for mobs of people to use the social internet to dismantle the lives of anyone believed to have harmed someone else, even when *harm* is defined as loosely as "disagreement." No matter how offended we are by someone's actions on the internet, we must not believe the lie that "we must dismantle the lives of harmful people." It is unacceptable for anyone, let alone followers of Jesus, to destroy people we have wrongfully demonized because of views or actions we find objectionable.

I want to leave this chapter with the words of Jonathan Haidt and Greg Lukianoff, who share profound words on cancel culture throughout *The Coddling of the American Mind*. In concluding one line of reasoning regarding cancel culture (or "call-out" culture, as they prefer to call it): "Life in call-out culture requires constant vigilance, fear, and self-censorship. Many in the audience may feel sympathy for the person being shamed, but are afraid to speak up."[4]

Let's not make people live in fear. Let's speak up for those who are wrongly shamed online. Let's work to clean up the poisoned water in which we swim, not add to its toxicity.

In order to do that, we'll need to take some intentional steps to step back from our immersion in the social internet and remember that there is much more to life than what happens in our feeds.

PART 3

Where Do We Go from Here?

CHAPTER 9

Study History

T he 2016 United States presidential election season was unlike anything I have ever seen or could remember from any history class I've ever taken. Regardless of whether someone liked the result of the 2016 campaign and election cycle, most everyone who paid any attention agreed that it took partisanship and political angst to heights we haven't seen in decades.

From my perspective as a social media manager, it was especially turbulent. It felt like everywhere you turned in the social media space there were land mines. A significant portion of social media users were seemingly out to start a fight whenever they logged on, and if you made one wrong step, you'd find yourself toe to toe with a mob of angry people who wanted to debate or demean you until you surrendered and promised to vote for whoever they wanted to win.

A significant reason the 2016 U.S. presidential election was so volatile on social media is because the candidates themselves were more outspoken and negative on social media than ever before, particularly the political newcomer, Donald Trump—a man seen as a political outsider who rallied the "common man" to take down the establishment of Washington. I remember many conversations about the state of social media discourse during this time ending with: "America has never seen anything like this before." But I learned that, actually, America *had* seen something like this before.

For all of the tumult that came with the 2016 United States presidential campaign and election season, there was one bright spot (other than the Chicago Cubs winning the World Series). *The Washington Post* created a podcast called *Presidential*, which explored the lives and work of each U.S. president over the course of a thirty- to fifty-minute weekly episode. It is still one of my favorite podcasts ever, and I highly recommend looking it up and listening.

Getting small snapshot biographies of each U.S. president lit a fire in me to eventually read a biography of every U.S. president someday. One of the episodes of *Presidential* that stood out most was the episode on President Andrew Jackson.

If you don't know about President Andrew Jackson, he served as the seventeenth president of the United States and is most famous for signing the Indian Removal Act in 1830 to displace Native Americans in an attempt to give white people more land. Jackson had a rough upbringing, and it changed his entire life. He was a combative man, even in his young life, once dueling a British man and taking a bullet so close to his heart he could not have it removed for fear of it causing him to bleed out. Jackson was the first president who didn't come from the colonial elite class and campaigned for the presidency by advocating for the rights of the "common man" as an outsider.

Why do I tell you all of this? While many of us were reeling during the 2016 presidential election season, confused about why rhetoric had reached a previously unexplored depth of toxicity, wondering how to navigate a raucous sea of political and social realities we had never seen before, I learned that our situation wasn't actually unprecedented. In 2016 we witnessed a combative man branded as a political outsider pursue the office of president with the intent to represent the views of the common people who often feel neglected by political "elites." Andrew Jackson, though different from Donald Trump in many ways, helped me realize that though no one *alive* had ever experienced anything like what we were experiencing, our country had experienced this before. History helped me realize that, as the writer of Ecclesiastes says, "There is nothing new under the sun" (1:9).

This is the first chapter of several in which I want to provide you with tools to more wisely engage the social internet. It is too easy to passively swim through life, immersed in the dirty waters of the social internet, ignorant of how we arrived where we are and how to deal with our present circumstances. We must be vigilant and intentional about taking steps to slow down, zoom out, and carefully observe our lives so that we might resist the temptation to be caught up in the cycle of outrage, anger, and sensationalism that drives so much of what makes the social internet work.

The first intentional step I want us to take is to study history. It's easy for me to say, given that history was always one of my favorite subjects in school. But why is it important for us to study history? Allow me to give three reasons and then provide a few practical ways to do so.

Studying History Reminds You Nothing Is New

As I write this, the world is grappling with a slow return to normalcy in light of a pandemic. A "novel" coronavirus, a sickness in the same family as the common cold, originated in China sometime around the end of 2019, and brought the world to its knees by March 2020. This coronavirus is called "novel" because, while many coronaviruses exist like the common cold, the one that led to the 2020 pandemic has never been seen in humans before. A hallmark of consuming any sort of media in 2020 was hearing advertisement after advertisement repeat the same four words: "In these unprecedented times." The frequency with which we heard this phrase at the height of the pandemic makes my wife, Susie, and me laugh anytime we hear it now.

The reality is, though this strain of the coronavirus may be novel, enduring a pandemic is not. The events of 2020 were actually *not* unprecedented times! Multiple pandemics in the twentieth century alone took more than one million lives. In fact, the flu pandemic of 1918, which many have cited in comparison to the 2020 coronavirus pandemic, took an estimated fifty million lives.

Why does all of this matter in regard to our exploration of the importance of history? When we live in the moment, we can tend to feel alone in what we're experiencing. But, if we take a step back, zoom out of our own lives, and look at the broader time line of history, we realize that people have experienced circumstances like ours in the past. There really is nothing new under the sun. When we see that others have experienced situations like we currently experience, we can study them and learn from them in ways that may help us address our current circumstances, which leads to the next reason to study history. Realizing that others have experienced similar situations doesn't make our problems any less serious, but the realization that we are not alone provides some small comfort.

> When we live in the moment, we can tend to feel alone in what we're experiencing.

Studying History Helps You Solve Problems

When we take a moment to step outside our own life stories and examine the life stories of those who have lived before us, we recognize that nothing we're experiencing is unprecedented. When we recognize that our experiences aren't unprecedented, we can learn from the past experiences of others so that we solve whatever problems we face with efficiency.

At the beginning of this chapter, I mentioned the 2016 U.S. presidential election and how it created an atmosphere unlike any we had ever seen on social media. Misinformation and vitriol were stirred around in a cauldron of hatred and malice, and it felt as though no one could escape the rampant anger and negativity borne by the phenomenon. As rough as 2016 was for social media managers, it provided a helpful lens through which to view later election seasons—namely, the 2020 U.S. presidential election. On top of a raging pandemic, conflict about racial injustice, and a bevy of other contentious issues, a heated presidential election season ramped up at the end of the summer. What I experienced as a social media manager and common social media user in 2016 informed how I was going to approach the 2020 election season on social media.

How does this help us? It's pretty clear. When we take a moment to stop, zoom out, and examine history (or even just our own past experiences), we can learn how best to solve and avoid problems in our current context. Resist the temptation to think no one has experienced what you are experiencing. Discover people who have, and learn from what they did.

Studying History Broadens Your Understanding of Reality

We all have our own worldviews, governed by what we hold dear, shaping how we process all of our life experience. Our worldviews are like the goggles through which we view all things. These worldviews tend to be adjusted and fitted to our heads in our younger years, and once our first set of worldview goggles are set, it takes a lot to remove and replace them with a different set.

Most of us, I think, have our worldview fitted and set in place by the time we're in our mid-twenties. Our faith, our family, our tradition, and our past life experiences all work together to form our worldview. It usually takes a major shift in more than one of those factors to change how we see the world, which is why people so rarely make a major worldview shift.

Having a worldview is unavoidable—everyone has one. Unfortunately, having a set worldview makes us vulnerable to a precarious pitfall: tunnel vision. Holding a firm worldview isn't wrong, but when our worldview blinds us to the reality that not everyone views the world in the ways we do, we set ourselves up for failure.

I am a Christian, which means I think that a trust in Jesus Christ for salvation from my sins should be central to how I see the world. I also think that any worldview not ultimately built on this truth lacks in some serious ways. But these beliefs I hold do not, and should not, prevent me from recognizing the worldviews of my Muslim neighbor or my atheist friends. We can *recognize* others' worldviews without *validating* them. This is important to forging the bonds of friendship and seeing people who are different from us as human beings made in the image of God, not ideological opponents to be conquered.

Studying history allows us to temporarily take off our worldview goggles and don the goggles of someone else in history. When we wear someone else's worldview goggles, our understanding of the world broadens. For example, because my worldview is shaped by the fact that I am a white man born into the late twentieth century United States of America, I grew up with the belief that the Native Americans who lived in the Americas at the time of Christopher Columbus were a scattered, agrarian people who lived off the land like the Native Americans depicted in movies like *Pocahontas*. This misrepresentation gave me a narrow view of the world. But when I read *1491* by Charles Mann just a few years ago, I learned that many Native American groups actually erected great cities all around the Americas, living in close proximity, and they weren't just living in wigwams in the woods all the time like many movies portray.

Many of us may be afraid to study history because we're afraid of learning that we have been wrong about something (or many things) throughout our lives. View this as an opportunity, not a threat! Studying history helps us see the world through the eyes of others. This helps us empathize and love other people even when we don't agree with them—a practice poisoned by the sensationalism of the internet.

Own Your Education

How can you study history if you're not in school anymore taking history classes? It's simple: own your own education! Read, listen, and watch. Read books about the lives of others in history, or who are currently living, who are not like you. This helps you see the world through the eyes of other people, which is good even if you conclude that they view the world in some warped ways. Listen to podcasts like *Presidential* or others that give you perspectives beyond your own. Watch movies about real-life events, or better, watch documentaries that tell the stories of real-life events.

It can be difficult to know which resources to trust as you attempt to study history. To be honest, there is no such thing as an "unbiased" author or podcaster or other sort of history teacher. This is why it is so important to read widely and not just one sort of perspective. Likewise, try to consume history resources that provide evidence of any claims they make. If some author makes a claim in his book that George Washington had three secret wives, you should probably not take that as fact until you check any sources that may be provided. Discernment is important as you study history, and as mentioned before, no one is truly unbiased. But read widely and don't believe wild claims without any sort of evidence.[1]

When we are willing to study history, we are better for it. We realize nothing is new under the sun. We learn how to solve our current problems based on the past experiences of others. We learn that people see the world in different ways because of their faith, family, and experiences.

How does all this pertain to social media? At the end of the day, a better understanding of history helps us empathize with others. When we realize that nothing we experience is unprecedented and that well-meaning people who disagree often simply see the world in different ways, we can engage on the social internet in ways that are empathetic and loving, rather than defensive and mean.

CHAPTER 10

Admire Creation

I am an amateur bird-watcher. I use the term *amateur* as loosely as possible. What I mean when I say I am an amateur bird-watcher is that I have more birdhouses and bird feeders than the average person, and I make a concerted effort to sit, watch, and attempt to identify the birds that float between the houses and feeders in my backyard.

My favorite recent addition to my repertoire of bird-watching paraphernalia is the window feeder affixed to my home office window. My pest control guy says it will probably attract ants because the birdseed drops next to the foundation of my house; but that's fine because it also attracts birds—*lots* of them—and it allows me to see them mere inches away from my face.

I recently learned that Christian theologian and author John Stott was a bird-watcher—a real one, unlike me. Stott traveled widely during his life and ministry, and he would make time to observe birds throughout his travels. He worked to develop a new branch of science that he dubbed "orni-theology" or the theology of birds.

A couple of years ago, I came across a lesser-known John Stott book called *The Birds Our Teachers*, which is filled with bird photographs taken by Stott and eleven chapters of orni-theology, each explaining how different features of birds and bird life point us to the greatness and majesty of God. Stott admired creation and sought to better understand God through his creation.

A lot of my career has largely been spent looking at a screen, monitoring social media, and resolving conflicts that arise through the social internet. Such work is often filled with conflict, urgency, and lots of unnatural light. Bird-watching, and admiring creation in general, is integral to my life because it is everything my work is not. Admiring creation is slow, not urgent. Admiring creation requires no batteries or screens. Admiring creation is free of drama and conflict (except when mockingbirds get into it, as they occasionally do).

You may not work in front of a computer screen like I do, but you likely spend enough time on the social internet that it is shaping the way you think, the way you feel, and the way you see the world. Just as stepping back and studying history can give you perspective of your fast-paced online life, stepping back and admiring creation can do the same. In order to push back against the negative consequences of always being online and being constantly connected to others, we have to take intentional steps to engage in activities that are the polar opposite of the rhythms that drive our lives.

Why is admiring creation an important part of learning to live a more off-line life? Let's explore three reasons.

Admiring Creation Makes Us Slow Down

I am blessed to live about a half mile away from a city park that is home to eight baseball fields, a couple of playgrounds, one of Tennessee's best frisbee golf courses, and about 475 acres of woods that contain seven miles of paved and unpaved walking paths. Susie and I didn't even know it was beside the neighborhood when we bought our house. Most days, when it isn't frigid or raining, we walk from our house to the park and do a few laps on the path around the baseball fields. On the weekends, when we have a bit more time, we often try to walk some of the paved paths in the woods.

I cannot overstate how much the routine of these walks has provided for me. We take them most often at the end of my workday before we make dinner and spend time together in the evenings. It is sort of like a "mental commute" for me as I detach my brain from a long day of work and transition into an evening of time with family and/or friends. It gives Susie the opportunity to share about her day, too, and it serves to get us on the same page after we've spent much of the day in the same house but not together. Our walks aren't fast—we usually walk about three miles in just under an hour—but that's sort of the point. It's a bit of exercise, to be sure, but it isn't meant to be a "workout" full of high-intensity movement and clanging weights.

Our evening walks serve a variety of purposes, but for me they serve as a reminder to slow down and appreciate the real, unpixelated life all around me.

All of us spend an inordinate amount of time engaging with family, friends, and foes online. Whether or not your work requires you to spend time on social media, you likely spend a significant amount of time scrolling and engaging with content. One estimate says Americans spend between two and three hours per day on social media—that's enough time to be a part-time job.

Life moves fast on the social internet. Content appears and then is gone, either removed by a mysterious algorithm which has decided it is too old to be interesting or bumped down by a steady stream of more recent content. Friends share all of the most interesting or impressive parts of their life. We constantly "just check" our favorite social media platforms to be sure we don't miss anything our friends have posted because if we go too long in between checking in we may miss something. How tragic that would be!

> When we spend more time admiring creation and less time clicking "like" on the photos of others' lives, we enrich our own.

When we spend more time admiring creation and less time clicking "like" on the photos of others' lives, we enrich our own. Enjoying creation is an activity meant to turn down the speed dial of our lives, remove us from the hamster wheel of social affirmation, and point us to what really matters. Slow down and don't just smell the roses but see them, touch them, and hear the bees buzzing between them.[1]

Admiring Creation Engages All Five Senses

When considering the practice of admiring creation, the focus is rightly on, well, *creation*. We think of admiring creation in terms of observing beautiful birds, stargazing, or tending a backyard garden. This is all well and good, to be sure, but I think an overlooked feature of admiring creation is what admiring creation *does to us*. Admiring creation can often engage all five of our senses at once, helping us experience the fullness of life in a way scrolling through Instagram while watching Netflix simply does not.

We were created to touch, smell, see, hear, and taste. I fear that many of us, myself included, are missing out on much of life because the screens in front of which we spend a disturbing amount of time only engage our senses of sight and hearing. When we set our phones aside and take time to enjoy creation, we experience the fullness of our senses in a way that scrolling on Twitter or watching YouTube videos simply cannot. We can smell fresh-cut grass. We can taste ripe, just-picked apples. We can smell rain as it makes its way to our backyard to water our magnolia trees and their new, fragrant blooms.

One of the major pitfalls to being consumed by the social internet and spending hours scrolling and "just checking" our phones every day is that we neglect a few of our senses and miss out on so much of the beauty around us. Instead of appreciating the beauty in our backyard, we long for the beauty we see as we meander our way through the virtual wax museum of Instagram or yearn for the perfect family we see in photos on Facebook. There is beauty all around us, and we have five different ways to experience it—if we would just set down our phones and go outside. One of the problems, though, is that the social internet has warped our understanding of beauty in such a way that the magnolia blooms in our yard don't look and smell as remarkable as we ought. What tragedy has befallen us when we believe the real world pales in comparison to the worlds we have constructed on our screens!

> When we set our phones aside and take time to enjoy creation, we experience the fullness of our senses.

Admiring Creation Reorients Our Ideas of Beauty

It's no secret, nor is it really questioned, that the social internet has mutated our understanding of what is "beautiful." The primary culprit in this mutation is Instagram, the most popular, visually driven social media platform on the planet. When Kevin Systrom and Mike Krieger set out to create Instagram, it was meant to be a simple app that took advantage of the new cameras being installed on smartphones. Filters were provided for artistic flair and to mask the relatively low quality of the early smartphone cameras. Systrom, the more artsy, creative founder of the duo, has particular tastes in basically everything. For instance, he drinks only the highest quality coffee, purchases the choicest wine, and seeks out only the most talented, brilliant mentors. He wants everything he does to be the best, and he's pretty obsessive about it. Sarah Frier writes in her book *No Filter*, which chronicles the story of Instagram, that Systrom's dad once bought him a baseball, bat, and mitt to teach him baseball. Systrom asked if he could check out books at the library about how to play first. He couldn't bear trying baseball without first making sure he was doing everything perfectly.[2]

It is no wonder, no matter how unintentional it may be, that Systrom's app (Instagram) has redefined "beauty" in some unhealthy, obsessive, perfectionistic ways. Systrom created Instagram with the intent to provide an outlet for people to share the beauty of their lives on the internet and experience the beauty of others' lives through the same. But instead of Instagram being a virtual representation of off-line beauty, it has redefined what "beauty" is. What was created to be a sort of mirror for beauty has become a gatekeeper for it.

Instagram is no longer a mere virtual representation of real-world beauty. It has warped our understanding of what beauty is by creating a system in which beauty is defined by perpetual refinement, filters, and affirmation rather than raw, unfiltered, no-need-to-be-affirmed reality.

Instagram was created to capture beauty, not redefine it. Instead of being a place where people come to appreciate the magnificence of the world, Instagram gave us the tools to construct our own world—one that has so changed the definition of beauty that the real world could never compare. It is terrifying to see our virtual re-creations of the real world become more appealing than the real world itself. But like Bo Burnham said as I quoted him before: "The non-digital world is merely a theatrical space in which one stages and records content for the much more real, much more vital digital space."[3]

So many of us scroll Instagram and consume the content without thinking about how that mindless scrolling and double tapping warps our ideas of what is beautiful and remarkable. When we take time to set our phones down, go outside, and admire creation, we get to experience real-world beauty with our own eyes. Sadly, for many, our muscles for recognizing beauty have become so atrophied that even the prettiest sunset may not measure up to something we saw a friend post on Instagram. Or worse, we feel the need to capture a picture of the beautiful sunset we see and share it in order to receive affirmation from others, and, until we receive that affirmation, we cannot be sure it is *actually* as beautiful as we believe it to be.

If we have any hope to reorient how we understand beauty, there is really only one solution: we need to spend less time scrolling Instagram and more time admiring the beauty that is all around us in our own lives. If we want Instagram, or any other social media platform, to cease being the lens through which we see anything as "beautiful," we need to make the conscious decision to let our own eyes see and experience the beauty around us.

Take a walk around your neighborhood and note the different kinds of trees. Buy a telescope and find a dark, open field to view the night sky. Maybe buy a couple of bird feeders and become an amateur bird-watcher like me. Reorienting our eyes to appreciate the true beauty all around us requires intentionality, and we must first be willing to spend less time on the app(s) that have warped our understanding of beauty in the first place.

The Good We Miss

When people talk or write about the unhealthy addiction we have to the social internet, the focus is often on how the social internet negatively affects us—that's what this book is primarily about! But I think it is equally important to look not only at how the social internet negatively affects us, but also at the good we miss out on when we spend too much time swiping, scrolling, and staring at a screen. I hope this chapter has opened your eyes to what our hours of mindless scrolling have caused us to miss—the beauty all around us in our mundane, everyday lives. Don't let the social internet warp what you understand to be beautiful. Admire the beauty and creation all around you, and realize that no arrangement of pixels can ever match up to the smells, sights, and tastes of the real world.

CHAPTER 11

Value Silence

Growing up, I was a pretty talkative and outgoing kid. I wasn't ever really popular, but I made friends pretty easily and would occasionally get in trouble for talking too much in class. At the same time, I was a good student. Aside from a couple of high school math classes, I received all As throughout all my years of school, and I would regularly answer questions my teachers asked in class. But starting in about the eighth grade, when I began to feel the moodiness that teenagers feel as they begin the transition from childhood to adolescence, I tried something new from time to time, as a sort of social experiment.

Every now and then, maybe a couple of times a month, I would decide that I would spend a couple of days at school not saying *anything*. I would call them my "silent days," and they sort of weirded my friends out. I remember people asking, "Are you okay?," thinking something must be wrong if I wasn't talking. On those days I would sit by myself at the lunch table. I wouldn't talk to any of my friends unless they directly asked me a question. I wouldn't raise my hand in any classes.

Why did I do this? To this day, I'm not sure. Was it partially due to the sulking moodiness that comes with adolescence? Surely. Was it partially a brilliant understanding of the power of restraint and observation? Possibly. But I valued those days because every time I was silent, I learned so much. I used the time to study my friends. To pay close attention to the ways people interacted with one another. To learn how body language and other elements of social engagement played a role in relationships.

While it sounds a bit odd, I think the practice taught me that the world doesn't revolve around me and what I have to say and that other people are worthy to be understood and heard. It was an opportunity for me to remove myself from the center stage of my life, watch my friends, and learn how people worked without my own involvement in the equation.

Our Default Mode

We all have a knob on our hearts. Not literally, obviously, but figuratively. I imagine this knob on our hearts like a volume adjuster on a guitar amp or a speed adjuster for a ceiling fan. This knob has a default setting—a setting on which it begins and to which it will revert if it is not intentionally turned to a different setting.

As a Christian, I believe the default setting for the knob on our hearts is "sin." Because the default setting of our hearts is on sin, the path of least resistance for so many of the decisions we make in our lives will be one that, though easy to walk, produces brokenness and pain. It is easier to be selfish than it is to be selfless. It is easier to seek vengeance than to forgive. It is easier to be lazy than it is to work hard. Likewise, it is easier to be outspoken online than it is to be silent online.

Because our default setting is sin and brokenness, it appears to be totally normal and acceptable to be outraged on the social internet. Everyone seems to be doing it, so does it really hurt to join in on the rage?

Because the knob on our heart is set to sin and brokenness, we have to be *intentional* to change it to a different setting. The natural human approach to the social internet is characterized by anger and outrage, and resisting the natural, human, or "default" approach to the social internet requires *discipline.*

The social internet has given us a pocket-size soapbox on which to stand and speak up about whatever we like. It has never been more culturally acceptable to speak your mind and never stop pontificating on the issues of the day. All of us are so busy shouting at one another from our pocket-size soapboxes that we have lost the ability to listen over the din of our own voices.

Throughout this book we've talked of the social internet as "the water in which we swim," and we've recognized a variety of toxins in this water that are harmful to us. How might we recognize and attempt to remedy this other toxin—the nox-ious chorus of opinions slingshotting around online? Perhaps we should be silent from time to time so that we may listen, observe, and learn. Let's explore three reasons silence is valu-able, in general, and in relation to the constant noise of the social internet, in particular.

Silence Produces Empathy

Way back in chapter 3, we explored how the personaliza-tion of the social internet destroys empathy because personal-ization creates billions of different realities for each user. The personalization of the social internet is incredibly important to the companies who run the social internet because the more your experience is personalized to you, the more likely you are to continue spending time on their platforms. But this person-alization has created a situation in which we all live in our own little virtual worlds, receiving different diets of content, and we lack the ability to see what others' worlds are like. Because we lack the ability to see the world through the eyes of others, it is difficult for us to empathize with them and understand why they think and live the ways they do.

When we take time to be silent on the internet, refrain-ing from shouting our opinions from our pocket-size soapbox, we create a space in which we can observe what others are shouting about. When we take time to intentionally listen to the voices to which we are connected online, we can begin to empathize with them and attempt to understand why they think, believe, and speak the ways they do.

It is unnatural, it seems, to maintain a presence on the social internet and be silent. The chief appeal of social media is to call attention to our exis-tence, and to be silent works against that siren song. But the reason silence feels so odd is because the knob on our hearts is set to outrage, and our fingers do the bidding of our broken hearts. Silence requires inten-tionality. Silence sets us on the road to listening. Listening sets us on the road to empathy.

> The knob on our hearts is set to outrage, and our fingers do the bidding of our broken hearts.

Silence Encourages Wisdom

"Better to remain silent and be thought a fool than to speak and remove all doubt," is a classic quote on silence that is often attributed to Mark Twain, Abraham Lincoln, and others—though its origin is actually unknown, as there is no solid evidence for anyone famous actually saying it.[1] When we turn our knob off the default setting and attempt to be silent online, we create an environment in which wisdom can grow.

Listening to others and growing in empathy for them helps us see that the world doesn't revolve around us and our cares and that there may be legitimate ways to see the world beyond our own. By understanding that other worldviews and beliefs exist outside of ours, even if we don't agree with those beliefs and worldviews, we learn how others perceive the world and may make adjustments to how we live as a result. Though not biologically correct, it does seem that when our mouths are moving our ears are deafened.

Adopting intentional times of silence online can help us combat the lack of empathy being sown in our hearts by the feeling that we exist in our own little worlds, occupied by a select group of friends, family members, and news outlets who agree with us and tell us what we want to hear. When we have the courage to shut up, we unlock a world of wisdom that comes with listening more and talking less. It's amazing what we can hear when we aren't trying to listen to others over the sounds of our own virtual voices. Our ears, physical or virtual, have an easier time learning about the lives and experiences of others when we stop trying to be noticed ourselves.

But, in order to recognize the value that comes with listening to the experiences and worldview of others at the expense of constantly expressing ourselves, we have to recognize that the world, whether off- or online, does not revolve around us. This requires humility.

Silence Requires Humility

The entire next chapter of this book is dedicated to the importance of humility as it pertains to living our lives on the social internet. Our brief exploration of humility here at the end of chapter 11 is about humility's relationship with silence.

Why does silence require humility? Because silence requires us to recognize that we are not worthy of being heard any more than anyone else. A significant factor undergirding the fact that we all talk so much online is a belief—one we all hold—that we are the main characters of our lives and that everyone else in our lives is a supporting character. We view life this way because of the same default mode I explained before. When we believe life revolves around us, everyone else's opinions, cares, worldviews, and *lives* are less important than our own. What a selfish, sad existence—one that was certainly present before the invention of the social internet but has no doubt been enhanced by it.

But let's take care not to go too hard on this self-centered belief before we recognize that many of us are guilty of this perspective.

Being silent says, "What you have to say matters more to me right now than what I have to say." Listening to others says, "Your opinions and feelings and thoughts are as important as mine." This is humility in action. Humility requires us to remove our default bias that leads us to give ourselves the benefit of the doubt but not others, to believe our worst experiences are worse than anyone else's, to believe we alone and those who agree with us have a right view on life. Humility leads us to consider others as equally important as we consider ourselves, and more worthy of grace and kindness than we are. Humility recognizes that we are all supporting characters in our Creator's story and that none of us are stars of our own lives.

When we recognize that we are on a default setting of brokenness just like everyone else in our lives, we are more likely to be gracious and listen before we speak.

So What Then?

What do we even do? Is this a call to broody adolescent silence like I experimented with when I was a teenager? Not really, but I think my call to action may be a bit closer to that than you think!

What would it look like for you and me to spend more time listening on social media than we spend talking? Perhaps you currently post something on Facebook or Instagram once per day. What would it look like if you only posted once per week? Or twice a month? What if you vowed to only interact with others on Twitter if you had an encouraging word to share?

Our default mode is set to speak our minds as we please and listen to those with whom we agree. This default mode that governs our hearts is characterized by brokenness and what Christians call "sin." Let's commit to breaking out of the default mode in all kinds of ways, but especially in this way. Let's see what it would be like if people wondered where we went on social media. Let's make less noise, and let's work to intentionally listen to others so that we might learn who they are, what they value, and how their life may be different from ours. Let's have the humility to recognize that we aren't the main character of our lives and that we exist for more—namely, to love others and point them to the true Main Character of our lives.

CHAPTER 12

Pursue Humility

I have had the privilege of serving in student ministry since about the time I graduated from high school in 2009. Throughout college and since moving to Nashville, I have served in three different student ministries within three tremendous churches. I love helping students learn what it means to be a Christian and figure out how to follow Jesus. A big reason for that is because I remember well how volatile that time was for me, and I remember how God used a number of student ministry leaders to disciple me, encourage me, and teach me.

One of my favorite parts of teaching students about the basics of the Christian faith is helping them understand what all of the "Christianese" words they've heard in church actually mean. Every few years, if I have some influence in the content we are teaching students, I advocate for a series on Christian terms, what they mean, and what Scripture actually says about them. In such a series, we define terms like *grace*, *mercy*, *righteousness*, *holiness*, and more. These are all words you hear in sermons and church conversations, but often without much clarity regarding what they actually mean. *Grace* and *mercy*, for example, are often used interchangeably despite being very different concepts! Grace is provision of a gift or reward we did not earn. Mercy is the withholding of consequence or punishment we did earn in our disobedience. One of the terms I love to spend some time picking apart with students is *humility*.

What Is Humility?

A lot of us misunderstand humility to be self-hatred. A great quote on this misunderstanding from Rick Warren (often misattributed to C. S. Lewis), goes like this: "Humility is not thinking less of yourself, but thinking of yourself less."[1] When I was in high school, my student pastor taught us: "Humility is understanding who you are in light of who God is." I'm not sure if he got that from someone or came up with it himself, but I think it's helpful.

These two maxims about humility have guided my understanding of the principle throughout my adult life. We are not called to self-hatred. In fact, self-hatred can be a form of pride, as the self is the focus of the thought! The point of humility is to recognize who we are in light of who God is—that is to say, feeble, broken humans—and focus on the good of others rather than the good (or flagellation) of ourselves.

If humility has an antonym, it is pride. Pride is when one thinks too highly of oneself, as if one can do no wrong. Or, in accordance with Warren's idea, pride can simply be thinking about oneself too much, whether as good or evil! Where a humble person sets out to serve others and receive no glory or recognition, a prideful person sets out to save others and receive all glory and recognition.

If we are to effectively push back against the darkness of the social internet, we must recognize that pride is integral to so much of the dysfunction we find online. A simple unwillingness to admit wrongdoing undergirds much of the persistent conflict that can make spending time on the social internet emotionally taxing and perpetually discouraging. For all sorts of reasons we've already explored in this book, the social internet brings out some of the worst in us. Antagonism thrives on the social internet more than protagonism. Conflict drives engagement, content with lots of engagement spreads the quickest, and, thus, conflict is ever-present and inescapable.

How much better might our experiences online be if large groups of people committed to value humility? What if people

> Pride is integral to so much of the dysfunction we find online.

admitted they were wrong? What if people didn't let fear lead them to tear others down? What if we encouraged others rather than seeking attention for ourselves?

What is to stop you and me from being the people who start such a movement? How might we demonstrate that humility is valuable through our engagement online? Let's look at a few ways.

Let's Admit When We Are Wrong

A running joke among those who work in social media, and even among those who don't, is that no one has ever been convinced to change their mind because of a social media argument. This is likely not true, as surely someone has changed their mind at some point because of an interaction they had with someone else online. But the next part of the joke is that if someone *has* changed their mind because of an argument on Twitter or in the Facebook comment section of a news article, they almost certainly *never admit* it.

I am convinced that pride, generally, and the unwillingness to admit we are wrong, specifically, are at the heart of so much of the negativity that has come to define our experiences on the social internet. How radical would it be, then, for you and me to admit we are wrong when we're engaging with others online? Imagine the shock when you're debating a controversial issue in the comment section of a Facebook article and you eventually type, "You're right. My viewpoint is inconsistent," or something to that effect.

However, it needs to be noted that in order to have the courage it takes to publicly admit you are wrong, you need to actually have the capacity to think you can be wrong and sometimes make mistakes. This is a heart issue that runs deep beneath what we do or do not say on the internet. You're never going to admit you're wrong on the internet if you can't even do it among your family, friends, or coworkers. Pride is difficult to shake, and it starts with recognizing who we are in light of who God is. When you remind yourself that you are a mere human, and not a god among men, it becomes a bit easier to recognize that you are fallible and can do wrong.

Let's Assume the Best of Others

In addition to admitting when we're wrong, we should assume the best of others. But this is incredibly difficult to do.

As one who has spent most of his career monitoring activity on a wide variety of social media platforms, I am the first one to say that people are often the worst versions of themselves online. I've seen too much negativity and nastiness over the years for it to be remotely easy for me to give others the benefit of the doubt and assume the best of them. Numerous times I have been duped by commenters who claim to want help with a problem only to have them use the open line of communication to berate the organization I represent and everything we stand for. All of that is to say: I get why it's easy to be negative and cynical online.

Assuming the best of others on the social internet is hard because of the point we just discussed: no one admits when they are wrong because they're always driven by their pride and the desire to save face. I am calling you to be different. Let people fail you and hurt you before you assume that their motives are impure. The apostle Paul writes in Romans: "If possible, as far as it depends on you, live at peace with everyone" (12:18). If you're reading this as a follower of Christ, be reminded that we are to seek peace with others and engage in fruitful dialogue online even if it appears the others are out for virtual violence and digital blood. Assuming the best of others will make you vulnerable and open you up to being hurt. But is that not the price of a life defined by true love for others?

When we assume the best of others, we can prevent a good deal of conflict—so much of which is ignited when we assume someone is engaging with an antagonistic intent rather than a genuine, humble one. If we assume others on the social internet are acting in kindness, we may still find ourselves in some conflict, but believe it or not, this is actually a good place to be. Conflict will never leave the social internet because conflict will never leave human society. But when we assume the best of others and give them the benefit of the doubt, we are doing our part to prevent unnecessary conflict, as far as it is within our power to do so.

Let's Forgive Others When They Wrong Us

When we are inevitably wronged and hurt as we assume the best of others on the internet, let's be quick to forgive those who hurt us. Now, I want this book to be accessible for Christians and non-Christians alike, and I've been careful to write it as such, but this is where I have to speak directly to my brothers and sisters in Christ. You and I, friend, have no reason not to forgive! We are compelled to forgive because of how God has forgiven us. Since Jesus was killed so that we might be forgiven for all the ways we grieve the God of the universe, how can we deny anyone who hurts our feelings on the internet that same forgiveness? To refrain from dispensing forgiveness would be the height of hypocrisy!

Forgiving others requires a tremendous measure of humility. It requires humility because it requires us to recognize that we are not gods, or any higher level of being than our fellow man, and that we are just as capable of committing the wrongdoing to others that has been committed against us. There is great power in being offended, holding onto a grudge, and withholding forgiveness. A power to refuse to mend a broken relationship. A power to demand compensatory action from the offending party. A power that makes us feel *just* a little more godlike than we do without it. But to forgive is to release that power from our grasp and to be reminded that we are no more godlike than any other person. For when we forgive, we may no longer hold the offenses committed by the other against them, and we lose the power that is present in withheld forgiveness. This takes humility because it requires us to recognize that we are no better than the one who has grieved us.

No algorithm is engineered to promote reconciliation and forgiveness.

Forgiveness is desperately needed in the world of the social internet. As we have explored throughout this book, conflict thrives on the social internet. Conflict is engaging, and that which gets engagement is perpetuated by algorithms engineered to generate virality. Forgiveness is the antithesis of conflict. No algorithm is engineered to promote reconciliation and forgiveness. All algorithms are engineered to favor the spread of conflict and argumentation. This means forgiveness requires intentionality and will receive little fanfare. But if we value humility, fanfare is of minimal importance.

We Cannot Do It Alone

Because of the inherent brokenness in all of us, our default setting is to pride and not humility. To be humble anywhere, let alone online, requires tremendous discipline and intentionality. No one coasts into humility. We coast into our default mode—pride, protection, and the promotion of ourselves. If we hope to value humility in our online (and off-line) interactions, we have to *choose* to be humble. We have to actively ask ourselves: "How can I handle this situation with humility and not pride?"

Because this takes otherworldly discipline and intentionality, we have to recognize that we cannot do it alone. For thinking we can shake pride and pursue humility without any help is itself a form of pride, isn't it? We need family, friends, and colleagues who exceed us in maturity and their own pursuit of humility to come alongside us, spur us along when we get stuck in the mud, and encourage our hearts when we are discouraged by our repeated failure.

CHAPTER 13

Establish Accountability

How does the word *accountability* make you feel? What does it bring to mind? Does it make you feel excited to meet with a friend over coffee? Nervous because you have to answer for a way in which you have sinned or otherwise failed? Does accountability bring to mind maturity and discipline or conflict and shame?

Perhaps you feel a little bit of all of those feelings, which is where I am. Over the years I have had a variety of accountability partners or other kinds of relationships that acted as systems of accountability for me. The nature of those relationships has varied based on my maturity, the people involved, and a whole host of other factors.

Regardless of what your past experiences may be with accountability, I cannot overstate the importance of accountability as it pertains to our online activity and our online lives.

It is perhaps harder today to pretend that the social internet is its own little world like it used to feel in the late 1990s and early 2000s. It used to be much easier to sneak away and maintain anonymity, but today, because the internet is more commonly integrated with our real, off-line lives, hiding is harder and accountability is easier.

Don't get me wrong, there are still plenty of places to hide and pursue all manner of foolishness on the internet, but most of our social media platforms incentivize using our real identities, and our actions are more easily monitored and held accountable than they were in the earlier version of the social internet that was characterized by rampant anonymity.

As we have already explored at length throughout this book, the internet is governed by the attention economy. The primary currency of the social internet is attention, and the more attention we accrue, the more fulfilled we feel—as fleeting as that fulfillment may be. The easiest way to accrue this attention currency is by being mean, causing controversy, or engaging in outrage culture. My hope is that if you're reading this book, whether or not you consider yourself a Christian, you would want a friend who can come alongside you, hold you accountable, and let you know when you've been transformed into a more toxic version of yourself because of your relationship with the social internet.

We are weak, and that's okay! Weakness is nothing about which we should be ashamed. We just cannot ignore our weakness and willingly fall into destructive patterns that the algorithms governing the social internet set us up to adopt. We need help. We need accountability. Let me provide three reasons I think accountability is vital for us and our online activity.

The Benefits of Accountability

Accountability Keeps Us Humble

Assuming you're reading this book from front to back, we just came out of an entire chapter on the importance of pursuing humility in all of life, but especially as it relates to our online activity. So, if you remain unconvinced of the value and role of humility in our engagement with the social internet, I encourage you to reread the last chapter. But what does *accountability* have to do with our pursuit of humility?

Accountability reminds us of our weakness . . . in a good way. Accountability reminds us that we cannot will ourselves into maturity, wisdom, and self-control. We need help from other people. Recognizing weakness is a sign of strength. Ignoring weakness is a consequence of weakness. When we have the self-awareness to recognize that we are prone to believe one or more of the lies we identified in part 2 of this book, we should also realize that we need the help of trusted friends and mentors to keep us in check. What better example of pride is there than someone who is unwilling to receive constructive critique from a trusted friend? If you surround yourself with people who always affirm you and never tell you you're wrong, you're bound for greater troubles than using social media poorly.

Part of the deep brokenness in all of humanity is that we are actually *blind* to our brokenness and need others to help us see it. It is hard for many of us to come to terms with this because, for those of us who have grown up in American culture, needing help is a sign of weakness, and weakness is looked down upon. Even Christians look down on weakness despite the repeated theme throughout Scripture that God works through weakness, smallness, and those who may appear insignificant in the eyes of the world.

> If we have any hope to resist being caught up in the pervasiveness of pride online, we need people to come alongside and help us.

Pride runs rampant on the social internet; virtually no one ever admits they are wrong. At the same time, just about everyone who pridefully struts around online would say that they find pride repulsive and humility attractive. This is a picture of our broken state. If we have any hope to resist being caught up in the pervasiveness of pride online, we need people to come alongside and help us.

Accountability Guards Our Hearts and Minds

Spending lots of time on the social internet can be discouraging. Whether you simply observe the widespread negativity or find yourself participating in it, it is common to set down your phone feeling more emotionally and mentally exhausted than you were when you picked it up. Likewise, extended participation in the social internet can result in being molded into the image of the people and accounts you engage with. For instance, if you're constantly on Facebook, and your Facebook feed is filled with political ranting and angry discussions, you are likely to adopt those practices yourself.

We only ever think about the mark we are making on social media, but do we ever think about the mark social media is making on us?

It is not a coincidence that mental health statistics are growing more discouraging as social media use is increasing. If we are to resist the negative effects engagement online has on our hearts and our minds, we need help.

Part of establishing accountability as it pertains to our social internet use is the importance of having a friend or two who can keep us in check when we are being foolish. But another important part of establishing accountability is to help us guard our own hearts and minds. It is easy to log on to our favorite social platforms every day and not think about how those platforms are shaping us. Our mental, emotional, spiritual, and physical health can deteriorate quickly, without our even realizing it, simply because we are too online. We can be blind to the foolish ways we are using social media and blind to the ways social media is negatively affecting our hearts and minds. This is why establishing a relationship of accountability with a trusted friend or group of friends is important.

An accountability relationship can guard our hearts and minds against the harmful effects of extended social media use because friends are more likely to see downward trends in our health than we are. This sounds like a silly statement, but here it is: we are with ourselves every day. Because we are with ourselves every day, it is harder for us to see small changes in spiritual maturity, emotional stability, or mental health than it is for a friend who checks in with us once a week or twice a month. Likewise, because admitting a downturn in mental health or any other kind of health can feel like weakness—which is seen as bad in most contexts—we are likely to sweep under the rug any decline we *do* recognize in ourselves so we aren't ashamed when we talk to others about it.

A healthy accountability relationship is like a mirror into our souls. Sometimes we don't like what we see in the mirror, but without the mirror we would never see the way our souls are being shaped by the world around us. Such a mirror helps us guard our hearts and minds from the many detrimental effects of living our lives online.

Accountability Produces Discipline

Until sometime in high school, I didn't understand the difference between discipline and punishment. When you're disciplined as a child, it usually just feels like punishment. Parents recognize that sending a child to his or her room for disobedience may discipline and mature their child. But when you're a child, you don't view being sent to your room as a growing experience as much as you see it as a consequence for disobedience. But discipline is not punishment! Discipline is about growing in maturity and self-control. A significant part of growing in discipline is recognizing that our actions have consequences. The problem is that the same pesky blindness that keeps us from seeing our own foolishness and the negative effects of the social internet also prevents us from identifying the consequences of our actions.

Our brokenness, or what Christians call sin, blinds us from so much that we need friends to lead us by the hand through every aspect of life, especially our relationship with the social internet. When we have trusted friends who have permission to deliver firm words of correction, we are more likely to grow and learn how to avoid pitfalls. If we don't have friends who can deliver firm words of correction, we will fall into pit after pit of foolishness and never learn how to avoid them.

Practically speaking, when you have an accountability relationship, you are responsible to be open and honest about how you have failed. Only when you are open and honest about how you have failed can you grow. Without that openness and honesty, your accountability has no real means of fulfilling its purpose. But when you admit, for example, to your accountability partner, "I got in a fight on Facebook with my uncle last week," then the two of you can talk about that, why it was wrong, and how it can be avoided in the future. If admission of wrongdoings like that never happens, you're not going to become more disciplined and learn how you might avoid such pitfalls in the future.

We All Need Help

We are all helplessly blind to our own weakness, and we are conditioned by the culture in which we live to believe that weakness is something of which we should be ashamed. This produces a deadly scenario in which we repeatedly make foolish decisions, are negatively affected by the decisions of others, and have no means of growing in maturity and self-control. The reality is that, whether because of blinding pride or willful ignorance, most of us simply have not grasped the wide variety of ways in which our obsession with the social internet affects our lives. Human nature makes it difficult for us to see those effects with our own eyes—like trying to look at ourselves without a mirror. When we establish accountability, we set up a mirror so that we might have a better view of ourselves and how we are being shaped by our always-online lives.

Just as looking in a real mirror is not always a pleasant experience, neither is having conversations with those who keep us accountable. But we ought not avoid hard conversations because they make us uncomfortable, we ought to welcome them because they lead to humility and maturity. The social internet is an incredibly powerful tool that can be used for both construction and destruction. More often than not, we either wield it in destructive ways or are impacted by others wielding it in recklessness or with the intent to harm. Let's not fall for the lie that we can do it alone.

We could all benefit from a trusted friend or mentor with whom we could regularly meet and be open about our shortcomings. But establishing an accountability relationship is sort of "level two" of a friendship—we must first build real, off-line relationships. Your Facebook friends or Instagram followers are no replacement for real friends and off-line relationships.

CHAPTER 14

Build Friendships

ood friends are one of life's good gifts. Friday game nights with takeout Thai food and a lot of laughter. Comforting conversations over a cup of coffee following the tragic loss of a loved one. Long walks and talks in the park about the deepest depths of life itself. These moments are unmatched.

True friendship is often much stronger than the blood bonds that bring together families. True friendship requires selfless love, a willingness to endure conflict, and the ability to say what needs to be said. Friendship is terribly inefficient and inconvenient. In a cultural moment in which efficiency and convenience are everything, friendship seems like a distraction. It requires a sort of endurance and long-suffering that run against the ever-increasing speed of our daily lives. Friendship requires us to care for the good of others at least as much as, and hopefully *more* than, we care for our own good.

The social internet has cheapened friendship. Myspace allowed users to create "top friends" who were featured prominently on user profiles. Many millennials remember the "top friends" feature on Myspace serving as a battleground for adolescent social disputes. Friends, and particularly the ranking of them, became pawns in a vicious game of reputational chess. You could threaten friends with the horrifying idea that you would remove them from your "Top 8," in an effort to scare them into submission and loyalty. Facebook commoditized friends further through its perpetuation of much of the Myspace system, minus the "top friends" feature. Every connection on Facebook is considered a "friend," watering down the concept of what a "friend" is in our mind without our even noticing it. Today we use the word *acquaintance* as a synonym to *friend* because the concept of a friend has been robbed of some of its weight.

A healthy relationship with the social internet requires us to reclaim the real, deep understanding of friendship that has been lost. It is important to have real friends with whom we spend time in person. We have to resist the temptation of our screens becoming mediators of every relationship we have. Our screens mute the full range of friendship. A friend offering text-message condolences

> The social internet has cheapened friendship.

following the death of a family member cannot compare to their embodied presence and comforting embrace. A "happy birthday" message on Facebook just isn't the same as receiving a handwritten card from a distant friend. I think many of us have become so fused with our phones that we have forgotten the magic of real, embodied friendship. What value are these friendships?

The Value of Real Friendships

Friendships Remind Us of What Is Real

One of the more damaging effects of living life fused with screens and phones that we haven't explored in depth in this book is the sort of detachment from reality that happens when every part of life is filtered through a screen and a set of algorithms. The most prolific form of this phenomenon is the rise in popularity of false news. But our collective detachment from reality goes well beyond believing false narratives about what is happening in the world. That is a problem in and of itself, to be sure, but I think our detachment from real, embodied friendships is worse. When we don't connect with others in our off-line lives, we can lose our grasp on what real friendship looks like, what it looks like to live life alongside embodied people, as opposed to the "friends" we collect on our preferred social media platforms.

As we have already investigated at various points throughout this book: our online lives are real, but not *fully* real. So much of our online lives are curated and polished, lacking the raw, rough edges of off-line life. When we build friendships that primarily exist off-line, unhindered by filters of perfection or algorithmic manipulation, we are reminded of what is fully real. Off-line friendships are rooted in the deepest matters of life, while online friendships most often revolve around content, controversy, and rampant conflict.

Friendships Give Us an Opportunity to Sacrificially Love Others

The key to any long-lasting friendship is a desire to do what is best for our friends at all times, even when doing what is best for our friends may come at great cost to ourselves. This is sacrificial love—from a Christian perspective, this is demonstrated in the life of Jesus Christ.

Sacrificial love is the backbone of deep friendship. This doesn't mean we need to be constantly seeking out ways to put ourselves in harm's way in order to protect our friends—few of us will have the opportunity to "take a bullet," whether literally or metaphorically. Sacrificial love is usually much more mundane than that. Sacrificial love as the backbone of our friendships is most often seen in the simple acts of service we do for friends amid the rhythms and routines of daily life. It looks like babysitting a friend's kids for free while your friend and her husband go out for a much-needed date night. It looks like dropping off some Starbucks for a friend who has had a hard day at work. It looks like dropping everything you're doing to go for a walk with a friend who just needs to be with someone who loves them.

The sacrificial love upon which real friendships are built is incredibly difficult to enact on the internet. This is why incarnational, real-life friendships are so superior to online friendships. A friend you meet in a Facebook book club can make good conversation, but he can't come help you change a tire. A friend you make in the Instagram comment section of your favorite influencer can give you the best makeup tips, but she can't be by your side when you endure real tragedy and your tears are making your mascara messy. All of this is to say: making online friendships isn't wrong, but there is a sort of "ceiling" to them that cannot be crossed without regular off-line interaction. Embodied friendship can reach a level of intimacy that virtual friendship simply cannot, and the primary reason for that is sacrificial love that undergirds friendship is harder to express virtually than in person amid the rhythms and routines of daily life.

Friendships Encourage Us in the Darkest Seasons of Life

At no time is a friend more necessary than when life is difficult. An important part of friendship is *being* the friend that comes alongside your friend enduring a difficult season of life. This is an important manifestation of the sacrificial love we just examined. Equally important is being on the receiving end of the sacrificial love of a dear friend when *you* are the one enduring the dark season of life.

I experience this most clearly through the community group I lead in my church. Every Tuesday night a small group of friends comes over to our house. We share a meal, we talk about what is going on in our lives, we study the Bible, and we pray for one another. The people in this group truly love one another. As we have met over the years, we have learned more about one another and we have endured dark seasons with one another. We have hugged one another. We have sat and cried together. We have visited members of our group who move to faraway places. This group of friends embodies what it means to encourage one another in the hard times. We can't find this sort of relationship online. We may be able to find whispers of it, but no number of Zoom hangouts can replace spending time together in the same room.

I have a couple thousand Twitter followers. I have hundreds of friends on Facebook. None of those people have endured dark seasons of life with me like the people in my community group have. In past dark seasons, social media has been a helpful tool to ask for prayer or other means of support, but often the people who offer prayer or support through social media don't *really* know the lives and circumstances of the people for whom they are offering prayer or support. That doesn't make it wrong or bad—it's not wrong to pray for or support strangers—but tweets or Facebook messages of support during a dark season of life aren't the same as a friend's tearful embrace or quiet presence.

How Social Media Best Helps Friendship

While it looks like I have spent a lot of energy dogging the idea of online friendships, I think it is important for me to end this chapter by saying that online friendships are often constructive and incredibly fruitful. I do not mean to say the social internet is *only bad* for friendship—it isn't! One of my best friendships for years was built entirely through the internet. (Though, it should be noted, that friendship did not reach the level of lifelong best friendship until my friend and I happened to move to the same city.) Likewise, the social internet is a wonderful tool for keeping up with friends from my younger years, as well as friends who move away.

Here is how I would summarize how we ought to view the relationship between the social internet and our friendships: the social internet is best seen as a means of supporting the off-line friendships that are best suited to provide a means of sacrificially loving others. My fear is that we are so consumed with the social internet and making friends on social media that we neglect the real-life friendships available with people in our neighborhoods, our workplaces, or our churches. My hope is that we see social media not as a primary means of maintaining our friendships, but as a sort of "bonus" avenue to cultivate the friendships that primarily exist off-line.

If we spend too much time collecting virtual friends and building relationships with people we never see with any regularity, we rob ourselves of the sacrificial love we can give and receive in embodied friendships with those around us.

We would all do well to examine how we spend our time building friendships. Perhaps a challenge for us would be to tap our way to the dreaded "screen time" section of our phones to see how much time we spend on social media and compare it with the amount of time we invest in friends each week. My fear is that many of us spend ten to twelve hours a week scrolling our preferred social media platforms and only a small fraction of that in the physical presence of friends. What if we reduced the amount of time we spend mindlessly scrolling Instagram and increased the amount of time we spend having conversations about the deep things of life over coffee?

Real friendships are difficult because to love others more than we love ourselves is not natural. Real friendships require us to die to ourselves and consider the wants and needs of others before our own. Online friendships often make no such requests and, as a result, bear less fruit. Let's not deprive ourselves of the richness and depth of real friendship because we have decided to settle for an easier, more comfortable, cheaper brand of belonging.

Conclusion

The social internet is the most consequential invention in human history.

Of course, the light bulb, the telephone, and other inventions had to pave the way, so the social internet stands on the shoulders of other important technological advancements without which it would not have been possible. But what I mean more specifically is this: in the last anthropology class ever held in the history of the world, the social internet will be recognized as the fulcrum on which all human history shifted. The instant communication of ideas and information across the world and eventually across the solar system will have a more dramatic effect on any advancement that came before or will come after.

I know this sounds like an overstatement, and it may be, but I don't think so. The light bulb was important, but people didn't use the light bulb to topple governments. The telephone connected people in a way they had never been connected before, but it didn't connect people across the world in an instant.

We are in a difficult spot. We are some of the first people to learn to live with the social internet. People who come along in fifty or one hundred years may have it a bit easier in this regard, as the social internet will have had more time to work through its growing pains. Alas, we are living in the growing pains. We are having to learn to live in a world controlled by an invention that it seems we can no longer control. We made social media, and it is remaking us.

> We made social media, and it is remaking us.

At the Heart of It All

Why do I believe the social internet will be the most consequential innovation in human history? Because at the heart of the social internet is *people*. People are what make the social internet special and scary all at the same time.

People form the social internet, and, in turn, the social internet is forming people. This book has been my attempt to demonstrate that the social internet is likely forming you in more ways than you realize. When we post content online, we feel like we're making a dent in the world, that we're leaving our mark. I'm more concerned with the marks being left on us. The marks that may turn out to be scars.

A lot of people mistakenly believe the social internet is a neutral tool that has just been misused by bad people. A Christian may say, "Social media is not bad in and of itself, but sinful people use it in bad ways." This is wrong. Why? Because the same broken people who use the social internet every day also *created* the social internet. The social internet is not some neutral tool we discovered and started using poorly. The social internet was created by fallible—or in the Christian vocabulary, *sinful*—people who are broken in all the same ways as the people who abuse the social internet.

So, where does this lead? What is next? Allow me to make some predictions and look ahead at what is to come.

The Future of the Social Internet

One day, in the not-so-distant future, the last person who remembers life without the internet will die. What will the social internet look like at that time, in fewer than one hundred years? Let's look at some reasonable and wacky predictions.

A Mental Health Crisis

Some would say that the social internet has already caused a mental health crisis, and I am inclined to agree with them. But I think that, in the next one hundred years, we will endure a mental health crisis of pandemic proportions whose roots can be found in the sociological machinations of the social internet. Rates of depression, anxiety, and suicide will continue to rise to unimaginable rates, and the finger will be pointed at social media as the culprit. Global efforts will be undertaken to reckon with the mental health consequences of an online life we can't escape.

Government Regulation

At some point, likely soon, governments will start regulating some of these companies in some serious ways. Facebook, for instance, is already pleading for the U.S. government to step in and provide regulations for content moderation on their platform. Just as the Federal Communications Commission (FCC) currently regulates radio, TV, and other legacy communications platforms, the U.S. government will either set up a new service to regulate the social internet or expand the jurisdiction of the FCC to oversee social internet content. This process will almost certainly be complicated and inefficient, but I do think it is needed.

Even More Polarization

It may be hard to believe, but I think we have only scratched the surface of the polarization and discord that can be sown over time by the social internet. I believe that, in the next one hundred years, people of different ideologies will flock to platforms predominately used by people who share their worldview. This has already happened a bit, actually. Right now Facebook users trend more conservative and Twitter users trend more liberal, which makes sense given that Facebook is the largest social media platform in the world and Twitter is the favorite of academics and journalists. I think that, in the next one hundred years, people will gravitate to platforms based on shared ideology more than cool features.

But I do think there will still be platforms for people of diverse viewpoints as well.

War

In the next one hundred years, the social internet will be a primary factor in the initiation of at least one war, perhaps one on a global scale. Social media has already been used to manipulate elections and topple totalitarian regimes. In fact, this isn't a fair "prediction" because social media already led to some localized conflict in Myanmar in 2017, where Facebook was used to promote violence against the Rohingya people and the genocidal actions that were taken against them. The idea that the social internet would be used to initiate a global conflict is hardly far-fetched. If you think social media leading to a world war is a ridiculous idea, you may need to read this book again in order to understand that the same platforms you use to watch funny fail videos are also being used for political propaganda.

Final Words

What if we spent less time watching others live their lives and spent more time living our own?

What if we paid less attention to the incessant twittering of others and started paying attention to the beautiful birds singing their songs in our backyards?

What if we cared less about whether or not a high school acquaintance accepts our friend request and more about being the best friend we can be to the people around us?

What if we were less captivated by cat videos and paid more attention to the ways social media is warping the way we think, believe, and feel?

Perhaps then, we would be on our way to forming the social internet more than it forms us.

But first we must notice. We must pay attention. We must recognize that the water is toxic.

Notes

Introduction

1. Quote slightly modified due to explicit language. David Foster Wallace, *This Is Water: Some Thoughts, Delivered on a Significant Occasion, about Living a Compassionate Life* (New York: Little, Brown, 2009), 4.

2. Neil Postman, *Amusing Ourselves to Death: Public Discourse in the Age of Show Business* (New York: Penguin, 2005), 11–12.

Chapter 1: How Did the Social Internet Evolve?

1. Brian Livingston, "Cooking Up a Windows Networking Strategy," InfoWorld: Windows, Supplement to *InfoWorld*, October 21, 1991, accessed August 16, 2021, https://books.google.com/books?id=2 j0EAAAAMBAJ&pg=PA83&dq=windows+million+copies&hl=en&s a=X&ei=qYKIUcvIJ4_liwLU04HQBQ#v=onepage&q=windows%20 million%20copies&f=false.

2. Chris O'Malley, "Windows 95 Mania," Popular Science, December 1995, 27, accessed August 16, 2021, https://books.google. com/books?id=7n5BWbJWMXMC&pg=PA27&dq=windows+million +copies&hl=en&sa=X&ei=xYSIUbavMMOXigLKjYFI&ved=0CDcQ 6AEwATgU#v=onepage&q=windows%20million%20copies&f=false.

3. Tim Wu, *The Attention Merchants: The Epic Scramble to Get Inside Our Heads* (New York: Vintage, 2016), 207.

4. AOL offered unlimited email to all users, which drove growth on the platform early on, as Prodigy charged users extra for sending more than thirty(!) emails a month.

5. Joanne McNeil, *Lurking: How a Person Became a User* (New York: MCD Books, 2020), 67.

6. Because of space and time, I don't explain the entire history of Facebook in this chapter. If you want to read a lot more about Facebook's history than I share here, especially what happened between 2003 and 2006, I suggest Steven Levy's book *Facebook: The Inside Story* (New York: Blue Rider Press, 2020).

7. https://www.bloomberg.com/news/articles/2018-06-25/value -of-facebook-s-instagram-estimated-to-top-100-billion

Chapter 2: How Does the Social Internet Work?

1. Joanne McNeil, *Lurking: How a Person Became a User* (New York: MCD Books, 2020), 39.

2. Joanne McNeil, *Lurking*, 65.

3. Asurion-sponsored survey by Market Research Firm Solidea Solutions conducted August 18–20, 2019 of 1,998 U.S. smartphone users, compared to an Asurion-sponsored survey conducted by market research company OnePoll September 11–19, 2017 of 2,000 U.S. adults with a smartphone.

4. Nicholas Carr, *The Shallows: What the Internet Is Doing to Our Brains* (London: Atlantic Books, 2020), 118.

5. Adam Alter, *Irresistible: The Rise of Addictive Technology and the Business of Keeping Us Hooked* (New York: Penguin, 2018), 39.

6. Alter, *Irresistible*, part 2.

7. Carr, *The Shallows,* 117.

8. Mike Allen, "Sean Parker Unloads on Facebook," Axios, November 9, 2017, accessed August 17, 2021, https://www.axios. com/sean-parker-unloads-on-facebook-god-only-knows-what-its-doing -to-our-childrens-brains-1513306792-f855e7b4-4e99-4d60-8d51 -2775559c2671.html.

9. Jeff Horwitz and Deepa Seetharaman, "Facebook Executives Shut Down Efforts to Make the Site Less Divisive," *The Wall Street Journal*, May 26, 2020, accessed August 17, 2021, https://www.wsj

.com/articles/facebook-knows-it-encourages-division-top-executives
-nixed-solutions-11590507499.

10. Horwitz and Seetharaman, "Facebook Executives Shut Down Efforts to Make the Site Less Divisive."

Chapter 3: How Does the Social Internet Affect Our Lives?

1. Jaron Lanier, *Ten Arguments for Deleting Your Social Media Accounts Right Now* (London: Picador, 2019), 77–86.

2. Steve Rathje, Jay J. Van Bavel, and Sander van der Linden, "Out-Group Animosity Drives Engagement on Social Media," May 15, 2021, accessed August 17, 2021, https://www.pnas.org/content/pnas/118/26/e2024292118.full.pdf.

3. Rathje, Van Bavel, and van der Linden, "Out-Group Animosity Drives Engagement on Social Media," 7.

4. Nancy L. Rosenblum and Russell Muirhead, *A Lot of People Are Saying: The New Conspiracism and the Assault on Democracy* (Princeton: Princeton University Press, 2020), 168.

5. Phillippe Verduyn, David Seungjae Lee, Jiyoung Park, et al., "Passive Facebook Usage Undermines Affective Well-Being," APA PsycNet, accessed August 17, 2021, https://psycnet.apa.org/record/2015-08049-001.

6. Philippe Verguyn, Oscar Ybarra, Maxime Résibois, et al., "Do Social Network Sites Enhance or Undermine Subjective Well-Being? A Critical Review," SPSSI, January 13, 2017, accessed August 17, 2021, https://spssi.onlinelibrary.wiley.com/doi/full/10.1111/sipr.12033.

7. Holly B. Shakya and Nicholas A. Christakis, "Association of Facebook Use with Compromised Well-Being," *American Journal of Epidemiology*, February 2017, accessed August 17, 2021, https://academic.oup.com/aje/article/185/3/203/2915143.

8. Lanier, *Ten Arguments for Deleting Your Social Media Accounts Right Now*, 97.

9. This *Psychology Today* article cites a number of such studies: Phil Reed, "Anxiety and Social Media Use," *Psychology Today*, February 3, 2020, accessed August 17, 2021, https://www.psychologytoday.com/us/blog/digital-world-real-world/202002/anxiety-and-social-media-use.

10. Jonathan Haidt and Greg Lukianoff, *The Coddling of the American Mind: How Good Intentions and Bad Ideas Are Setting Up a Generation for Failure* (New York: Penguin, 2019), 149.

11. Derek Thompson, *Hit Makers: How to Succeed in the Age of Distraction* (New York: Penguin, 2018).

12. *Eighth Grade* (2018) is an incredibly uncomfortable movie but masterful for that very reason. Burnham cast real eighth-graders and did an amazing job depicting what it's like to be a middle schooler today. The movie is appropriately rated R. Isn't it fascinating that a movie depicting the real-life experiences of the modern eighth-grader is rated as not appropriate for audiences under the age of seventeen? Poetic.

13. Quote modified due to explicit language. From "Bo Burnham Examines Social Media," *The Off Camera Show*, November 16, 2018, accessed August 17, 2021, https://www.youtube.com/watch?v=_XHRJJe2Kl0&ab_channel=theoffcamerashow.

Chapter 4: We Believe Attention Assigns Value

1. Lauren E. Sherman et al., "The Power of the Like in Adolescence: Effects of Peer Influence on Neural and Behavioral Responses to Social Media," *Psychological Science*, vol. 27.7 (2016): 1027–35, doi:10.1177/0956797616645673.

2. Tim Wu, *The Attention Merchants: The Epic Scramble to Get Inside Our Heads* (New York: Knopf, 2016), 206.

3. It is sort of crazy to think about the real possibility that the reason many people get junk mail today is because AOL sold their information to direct-mail companies decades ago.

4. "Status Update," *This American Life*, November 27, 2015, accessed August 18, 2021, https://www.thisamericanlife.org/573/status-update.

5. Shirin Sharif, "All the Cool Kids Are Doing It," *The Stanford Daily*, March 5, 2004.

6. Tim Wu, *The Attention Merchants*, 307.

Chapter 5: We Trade Our Privacy for Expression

1. Shoshana Zuboff, *The Age of Surveillance Capitalism: The Fight for a Human Future at the New Frontier of Power* (New York: PublicAffairs, 2020), 8.

2. Zuboff, *The Age of Surveillance Capitalism*, 11.

3. Zuboff, *The Age of Surveillance Capitalism*, 296.

4. "Editorial Expression of Concern and Correction," PNAS, accessed August 18, 2021, https://www.pnas.org/content/pnas /111/24/8788.full.pdf.

5. Robinson Meyer, "Everything We Know about Facebook's Secret Mood-Manipulation Experiment," *The Atlantic*, June 28, 2014, accessed August 18, 2021, https://www.theatlantic.com/technology /archive/2014/06/everything-we-know-about-facebooks-secret-mood -manipulation-experiment/373648.

6. Andrea Huspeni, "Why Mark Zuckerberg Runs 10,000 Facebook Versions a Day," *Entrepreneur*, accessed August 18, 2021, https://www.entrepreneur.com/article/294242.

7. I say, "As of the publication of this book," because Facebook privacy breaches happen so frequently that, by the time you read this, there could be another, more prevalent breach.

8. Rosalie Chan, "The Cambridge Analytica Whistleblower Explains How the Firm Used Facebook Data to Sway Elections," *Insider*, October 5, 2019, accessed August 18, 2021, https://www .businessinsider.com/cambridge-analytica-whistleblower-christopher -wylie-facebook-data-2019-10.

9. Facebook changes its platform all the time, so the best way to find a step-by-step process on how to get control of your privacy on Facebook is found by searching online for "privacy settings on Facebook" or something similar. Try to find guides from places outside of Facebook.

Chapter 6: We Pursue Affirmation Instead of Truth

1. Max Read, "5 Theories about Conspiracy Theories," *New York*, February 6, 2020, accessed August 19, 2021, https://nymag

.com/intelligencer/2020/02/why-do-people-believe-in-conspiracy
-theories.html.

2. Not that this has ever happened to me. :-)

3. To learn more about how the Pizzagate situation developed, check out this breakdown: Gregor Aisch, Jon Huang, and Cecilia Kang, "Dissecting the #PizzaGate Conspiracy Theories," *The New York Times*, December 10, 2016, accessed August 19, 2021, https://www.nytimes.com/interactive/2016/12/10/business /media/pizzagate.html.

4. Adrienne LaFrance, "The Prophecies of Q," *The Atlantic*, June 2020, accessed August 19, 2021, https://www.theatlantic.com/magazine /archive/2020/06/qanon-nothing-can-stop-what-is-coming/610567.

5. Ben Collins and Brandy Zadrozny, "Extremists Made Little Secret of Ambitions to 'Occupy' Capitol in Weeks before Attack," NBC News, January 8, 2021, accessed August 19, 2021, https://www .nbcnews.com/tech/internet/extremists-made-little-secret-ambitions -occupy-capital-weeks-attack-n1253499.

6. Bo Burnham, *Inside* (Netflix special).

Chapter 7: We Demonize People We Dislike

1. Greg Lukianoff and Jonathan Haidt, *The Coddling of the American Mind: How Good Intentions and Bad Ideas Are Setting Up a Generation for Failure* (New York: Penguin, 2019), 30.

2. Lukianoff and Haidt, *The Coddling of the American Mind*, 27.

3. Jean M. Twenge, *iGen: Why Today's Super-Connected Kids Are Growing Up Less Rebellious, More Tolerant, Less Happy—and Completely Unprepared for Adulthood—and What That Means for the Rest of Us* (New York: Atria Books, 2018), 154.

4. Nassim Nicholas Taleb, *Antifragile: Things That Gain from Disorder* (Random House, reprint edition, 2014).

5. Lukianoff and Haidt, *The Coddling of the American Mind*, 40.

Chapter 8: We Destroy People We Demonize

1. It should be noted that some differentiate between "call-out culture" and "cancel culture." I do not differentiate because, in the end,

they're ultimately the same thing. Some progressives identify "call-out culture" as effective cases of cancel culture, as a way to distance themselves from the term *cancel culture*, which has attracted a more negative connotation over time. We will work with the term *cancel culture*, but I consider the terms interchangeable.

2. Aja Romano, "Why We Can't Stop Fighting about Cancel Culture," *Vox*, August 25, 2020, accessed August 20, 2021, https://www.vox.com/culture/2019/12/30/20879720/what-is-cancel-culture-explained-history-debate.

3. George Orwell, *1984* (originally published June 8, 1949).

4. Greg Lukianoff and Jonathan Haidt, *The Coddling of the American Mind: How Good Intentions and Bad Ideas Are Setting Up a Generation for Failure* (New York: Penguin, 2019), 72.

Chapter 9: Study History

1. American history is my favorite sort of history to study. If you are looking for a place to start, I recommend David McCullough and Ron Chernow. Both are great historians and are widely respected by people of all political persuasions. I have read almost every Chernow biography that exists, and they're amazing (Hamilton, Washington, Grant, etc.). But they're hefty! Audiobook format is great for those massive biographies. If you want more recommendations, email me at chris.j.martin17@gmail.com.

Chapter 10: Admire Creation

1. I think God intends to teach us something through bees—flying, needle-wielding creatures that defy the laws of physics and can be a literal pain but also without which we would lose so much of the beauty that grows and flowers all around us.

2. Sarah Frier, *No Filter: The Inside Story of Instagram* (New York: Simon & Schuster, 2020).

3. Bo Burnham, *Inside* (Netflix special).

Chapter 11: Value Silence

1. Side note: so many quotes are attributed to Mark Twain with some measure of uncertainty that I think it would be hilarious if he never said any of the quippy truisms that are assigned to him and he actually just went around taking credit for others' goofy sayings.

Chapter 12: Pursue Humility

1. Rick Warren, Day 19, "Cultivating Community," *The Purpose-Driven Life* (Grand Rapids: Zondervan, 2013).